BEING OF
HUMANITY

Gravity of the Self

Veronique Bianconi

BALBOA
PRESS

A DIVISION OF HAY HOUSE

Balboa Press books may be ordered through booksellers or by contacting:

Balboa Press
A Division of Hay House
1663 Liberty Drive
Bloomington, IN 47403
www.balboapress.com
1 (877) 407-4847

Because of the dynamic nature of the Internet, any web addresses or
links contained in this book may have changed since publication and
may no longer be valid. The views expressed in this work are solely those
of the author and do not necessarily reflect the views of the publisher,
and the publisher hereby disclaims any responsibility for them.

The author of this book does not dispense medical advice or prescribe
the use of any technique as a form of treatment for physical, emotional,
or medical problems without the advice of a physician, either directly
or indirectly. The intent of the author is only to offer information
of a general nature to help you in your quest for emotional and
spiritual well-being. In the event you use any of the information in
this book for yourself, which is your constitutional right, the author
and the publisher assume no responsibility for your actions.

Any people depicted in stock imagery provided by Thinkstock are
models, and such images are being used for illustrative purposes only.
Certain stock imagery © Thinkstock.

Print information available on the last page.

ISBN: 978-1-4525-9961-8 (sc)
ISBN: 978-1-4525-9962-5 (e)

Balboa Press rev. date: 2/20/2015

"We must acknowledge that we are temporarily divided but eternally connected. We are one spiritual being craving to co-create in this transient universe. It is our collective quest."

Being of Humanity

Contents

PREFACE

"In trial or difficulty I have recourse to Mother Mary, Whose glance alone is enough to dissipate every fear"

- Saint Therese of Lisieux (doctor of the Church, Carmelite, 1873-1897)

This book is the sum of my life experiences and the connections I have had with some benevolent beings. We can call them angels, ascended beings, supernatural beings... Many names have been given to them, but of most importance to me wasn't to know their names but to connect with them, to have a relationship with this invisible world, which I always felt close to, like a subtle presence in the background of my reality. Yet they do interact with us all the time although we generally dismiss this communication by ignoring and denying their existence, simply because we think with our practical mind on any subject or situation. I must say that the practical mind is very helpful for any daily living task and to ensure that our possessions and finances are kept in order, so as to survive in this modern world. But when it comes to explain the meaning of mystical experiences this pragmatism goes out of the window, and trying to fit these rational thoughts to explain metaphysical manifestations would be just a way to drive our minds insane. No rational thinking can keep up with such a magnificent dimension. This is the realm of the soul - the connection with the source of love — the dimension of our higher selves in connection with this universe. This is simply the world within.

This book translates the communication with the Queen of Angels, from Mother Mary to my higher self. It is a moment of clarity which I have gained many years after the sumptuous vision I had of the Virgin Mary, but also with her support after several hard times in my life. I had witnessed many spiritual activities and interventions in this physical realm, which took me to write this book. This book is a pure expression of my higher self, and its vision on this world, our world...

Author
acknowledgment

The creation of this book has been quite a journey. This book didn't come so easy, and it feels in some ways like I have given birth to my child, after a bumpy and painful labor, though always through an amazing interaction with my higher self and other beings. A spiritual achievement which I wish will inspire people to share their own mystical experiences with the world. I truly sense that the time for us to reveal what lies in our hearts has come. To become transparent with the purpose, for a better interaction with each other and a greater understanding of who we are. Our testimonies are the proof that this supernatural realm does interact with us on a daily basis, but in order to bring this communication forth, we need to talk about it, we need to share it.

I am fully aware that I do not possess an academic degree as such. But I do believe this is also my strength, if someone like me can do it, then anyone can! Fundamentally, we are celestial beings, and the courage and determination to write this book came from the core of my being. I became what I like to call an intuitive writer. I like to express my relationship with the occult and divine realm. My belief is that it is not a requirement to be qualified as such, you just have to learn to listen with your heart. I believe that writing is a basic right and tool, to express who we have come to be in our society. So, I hope to inspire others to do the same, whom do not hold a specific qualification or any academic achievements, if this is what stops you to step up and speak up!

I did come across the same insecurities, just when I started to write. Nevertheless as soon as I tapped into the power of my heart, my desire to share this vision and dream became stronger than anything or anyone else's. What I do know now, is that you cannot stop the purpose unfolding within this world, this shift is beyond the understanding of our small self and ego.

Most of all, I want to dedicate this book to Mother Mary, my guardian in this world, and to thank all the magnificent beings in this universe who have been supporting me in this quest, this includes my family, friends and my wonderful partner. Also I am very grateful to the internet, and to all the people and companies who strive every day to bring the light upon the darkness of our minds, which, without their resources and visions, I would not be able to accomplish my purpose.

Introduction to my spiritual awakening

My experience with the supernatural or paranormal started when I was very young.

First of all, my mother told me that when I began to speak, I was telling her that every night a white lady was staying beside me. She stood by my bedside, during my sleep... According to my mother (as I was too young to remember) this white lady was benevolent and was caring for me.

Then a few years later what I do remember is that, from about the age of four, I was praying to the Mother Mary automatically every night before falling asleep. None of my parents were practicing their religion, and I don't recall them talking about God to me or even discussing about spiritual matters at that time, especially of Mary. I was never told to pray to any divine beings or even God. But somehow my heart and mind during that period was really connected to Mary, and up to now she has always been present in my life. This connection with the Virgin Mary amplified with time. In many moments of my life I've prayed to her, during my teens and my adulthood. When I talk to her, I know she definitely listens, because she always leaves a sign, a trace, to make her presence known to me.

So now I will tell you about my mystical encounters, which I had experienced when I was younger.

At the age of five years old, I had an out-of-body experience. One morning the feeling of hunger woke me up. I decided to get up and have my breakfast, but as I was about to get out of bed a kind of lazy feeling started to arise in me. I still remember my baby bed. It was a white bed with railings on each side, like a cot, so I decided to rest my head on top of these before getting up. Suddenly, without realizing, I was out of my physical body! I was floating and seeing myself from above my head... From that perspective I was looking totally still and thoughtful, although I knew that this person was me, it was simultaneously feeling like my spirit was staring at someone else... all of a sudden the pace started to accelerate, and while I was taken further away from my body, I commenced to feel frightened at seeing my bedroom's ceiling getting closer and closer. The idea of knocking my head and hurting myself began to grow, even though my physical body was actually still in my bed! It was like my mind didn't realize that. The fearful thought of injuring myself against the ceiling took me right back into my physical body. This fear of having to feel physical pain got me back in an instant.

Now let me tell you a story about my first direct encounter with the Virgin Mary...

I was about nine years old when I had the most revealing experience from the supernatural realm. I was in my mum's bedroom, still in bed finishing eating my breakfast. I stayed late in bed that day, as I felt slightly unwell in the early morning, so when she came back to see me and get my breakfast tray, she asked me how I feel. I told her I was feeling much better and that I will soon get up to stay with her in the living room. She looked at me with a smile and left the room. But as soon as she closed the door, everything changed around me... My whole reality shifted, I went from being in my mum's bedroom, to being outside in the air, spinning above my birth town in very slow motion and having standing in front of me... the beautiful Virgin Mary. Her skin was glowing so much that I could see subtle sparks shining through her complexion. She was wearing a beautiful Prussian blue veil with animated cosmic designs. Those designs were looking like planets and stars moving in slow motion on top of her shoulders. It was magnificent. The veil was long enough to cover her head and the rest of her body. Mary was there talking to me in a very peaceful way, while looking at me with her beautiful face. Her look was so tender, and at the same time I could feel a powerful focus on me. I could see her mouth moving with each word. The only problem for me was that I couldn't hear her voice... I had the vision without the sound...

I never knew what Mary told me that day.

This supernatural experience never left my mind. From that moment my quest to find out about this message began. It was engraved into my spirit, like a blueprint into my brain, and unconsciously I started to consider her interventions in my life.

I know that she is there when I need her. She supports me with self-healing, but also she gives her energy to the people around me.

For instance, the most intense interaction happened when I was nineteen. My mother became seriously sick. She began to lose her memory gradually, up to the point that one day she became unable to recognize me or any other member of my family. This really affected me, and it was hard to understand why this was happening to her. The doctors and psychiatrists couldn't really understand it either, and were unable to give us a proper diagnosis. They seemed to be surprised with this sudden degradation of her mind, especially at her age, as my mum was only in her early fifties. They came to a conclusion that she will never recover her memory, and that it was maybe the psychological consequences of all the emotional traumas accumulated in her life time. This could have shut down a part of her brain related to memory. My dad, who had always been with her, was devastated. I remember seeing him going to the hospital every single day, even after his night shifts. Sometimes he was taking the car in the middle of the night to drive away, to only come back in the morning looking like a zombie.

I couldn't believe what was happening to us. I grew up within the typical southern French family, and all my childhood's memories are beautifully positive and joyful. So it was for me and my brother a real emotional roller coaster. One night I was feeling so sad, that I became desperate for a miracle. I started to really pray to and yearn for Mary, I asked her to do something for my mother's recovery. I was crying and arguing with God. I was so unhappy and frightened by the whole situation. I felt unable to get over the sorrow. This fundamental pain was taking away my whole joy and love for life. So I deeply called to her from my heart space, I asked her to help my mother retrieve her mind.

The day after that, I went to the Virgin Mary's cathedral, named in French "La Vierge de la Garde" which is the main touristic site in the city of Marseille, and also its emblem. This is a sacred place, and people from Marseille go there to pray to her. They light up different candles to ask her for favors and blessings. My mother definitely needed her grace, so I lighted up a candle and prayed to Mary again. I remained in the heart of the cathedral for over two hours… the tears were rolling down on my face, I could feel a connection deep inside my heart…. She was there, assisting me through this process of deep sorrow and unconsciousness. After a while, the negativity eased up, her energy temporarily healed me, and so I decided to go to the grocery store. As I entered the store, the radio was playing a French song called *"Tu verras"*, composed and written by a very famous French Jazz singer called Claude Nougaro. The title of this song means *"You will see"*.

The chorus goes *"Yes you will see, you will see, everything will start again… Yes you will see, you will see, life is made for that, starting all over again… You will see, you will see"*.

I knew that Mary was speaking through those words to give me hope, but what I also knew was that it was a sign from her, her way to tell me a bit about the future… she had heard my prayer. A few days later, the hospital rang to tell us that my mother had retrieved her memory! We were overwhelmed with joy. We went to visit her the same day and, when we entered her hospital room… there she was, talking to her roommate like nothing had ever happened. She was out of 'nowhere land' and back to the 'here and now' with us after all those months. After a week she was discharged from the hospital. We couldn't believe it! The love that my father gave to my mother all these months had definitely been part of my mother's recovery. But deep inside my heart I knew that Mary was at work.

So you can argue that it could be a coincidence…
but even the doctors were shocked, and told us
that this was a MIRACLE, due to the sudden
change in her situation. They truly believed that
my mum wouldn't have been able to recover
as much, and so quickly. This is one of many
manifestations I have witnessed in my life, and
just to talk about it could be the creation of
another book.

Nevertheless I was still seeking the sound of
Mary's voice. I wanted her to tell me verbally
about the message. So all my life I have been
trying to understand the signs. I've read many
spiritual and religious books, and I even
practiced different religions for a while. I also
tried to forget about it by giving up all spiritual
or religious practices. I dedicated my life to my
egoistic world for some time. I tried to become
an academic learner, but all those attempts
never lasted or worked for me, it seems that
always something in my life put me back onto
the spiritual path, in a subtle or radical way.

Eventually I began to let go and acknowledge
my destiny… It was a bit like if I was

controlled by this invisible realm and being. But paradoxically, I never felt pushed to enter a specific religious order, it was up to me to seek my own path, which takes me naturally to choose the more relevant way to express my spirituality. It seems now that I was meant to write this book and many others, I suppose, as my life seems to unfold more and more onto the spiritual and metaphysical path. It starts to make sense to me why I never have been able to adjust to what we now call the old paradigm, and why I could never learn in the "academic way", simply because I was born in this time, the time of our greater shift.

The spiritual reality is being revealed to all of us. More of the secrets of our universe are revealing themselves, it looks like science and spirituality are gradually merging together, as they discover more things relate to each other. The history of our origins is now questioned, which redefine our social roles too. People have started to rethink the system, especially since the Internet, almost acting as the "nervous system" of our humanity bringing us to the edge of truth through disclosure. I believe this global communication has triggered this paradigm shift. As we can see, things are transforming in all areas of our lives, our financial system is breaking down, putting us on the edge of a monumental economic crisis; creating a greater gap between the rich and the poor, the powerful and the miserable. Relationships have been redefined by most of us, as finding a real compatible life partner becomes more and more necessary to survive in this time.

An increase in spiritual teaching and self-development take us to the realization that we must love oneself before any link with another, so, in this transition from seeking out to seeking in, we exchange our bodies for some emotional kick. We know that Love is the primary energy for life, somehow we are still struggling to connect with our being within to totally surrender to its Love. So we got into a sentimental partnership to compensate this lack, like a runner from the ego. I think for sure we can say that this old paradigm is falling apart slowly but surely, and to prove it you just need to watch the news.

But to come back to Mary, this was my most amazing encounter with the supernatural realm, and this celestial being has always looked after me and the people around me. She made me discover the spiritual language, the one that communicates with us and our spirits. During my quest, I experienced a lot of different things, and I came across to a lot of different people. I always felt like I was there for them at times… So much so that when I turned thirty, a deep feeling of wanting to serve and help others started to grow inside me.

I started to work in mental health, as an assistant occupational therapist, and then entered the National Health Service (NHS) where I was trained as a therapy technician in trauma and orthopedics, and then as a clinical/rehab support worker in general medicine, for the London community services. Even though I was learning a lot in my work, I still didn't want to qualify to a specific profession in the field of symptomatic medicine. I needed a more holistic view. I wanted to implement the spiritual aspect of healing, so I decided to train in holistic therapies, as an energy and body worker. I qualified as Thai yoga massage therapist, and as a Reiki and Theta healing advanced practitioner. But most of all, I just followed my heart's desires and intuition.

Since then I have been learning "the parallel knowledge" I have trained for the new world, without knowing. Mary was leading me to the fifth dimensional world coming ahead of us, as this transition revealed the urgent need for spiritual and physical healing. The intensity of this shift in our reality is stimulating matter with such strong vigor, that it is shaking up the whole collective consciousness.

Now I know that this book is what Mary said to me that morning. It emerges from my heart to my brain, I was expecting to hear a voice, but the sound of her verve came through words.

Simply, I wasn't able to understand the meaning of her visit and message when I was nine. I needed to face my own demons first, before I could quiet my mind to experience life from the heart space. In fact, it's like she buried a seed deep inside my mind, and let the hardship of my life water this gift, to let it grow over the years inside of me, for it only to blossom now onto the weave of my consciousness. As I cannot keep it to myself anymore, I am ready to converse to the world. After a long reflection, and even now while writing, it is clear that my higher self was to take me here, to disclose my deepest interaction with Mother Mary.

This book is there to speak to me but also to you, and whilst writing it a feeling of déjà vu is filling my being.

This book is the sound of her voice, and, you reading it, are the motion of her lips.

But the main topic of this book is about us, our humanity as a whole entity, ready to step up into this new reality, to connect to our higher potential and being. We are bound to become the higher self that we are meant to be.

This new paradigm is rising above the shore of the universe… changing our world. All together we represent the body of this humanity, ready to develop with the support and unconditional love of the divine source of life.

So I hope you will enjoy this metaphysical conversation, as much as I have enjoyed writing it. I wish you to connect to the main message, which is to start living our lives from our higher self, ready to connect with our greater purpose in order to reveal this beautiful being through the rediscovery of natural talents; to serve our humanity with joy, assurance and integrity.

For all of us, and all our ancestors who always found the most balanced path through hardship and darkness. For all those battles fought, all those books written, and all those words spoken… for the ones before us who had cleared the way in order to let our humanity grow in the greatest part of the mind during this golden age.

It is not for us to start another war, to create another enslaved society, or to follow another dogma… instead it is for us to learn from what has already been done and to evolve through the wisdom of our ancestors. It is for us to cultivate a compassionate behavior toward each other and start to know thyself. It is for us to use our talents and skills at the service of our dreams and for each other's well-being. We are now about to reveal the human's realm by unleashing the power of our hearts onto the collective path, for it to serve the best part of the mind, and to let it be flowed with love.

CHAPTER 1

GRAVITY OF THE SELF

Note that I will use metaphors and analogies in order to assist the mind with this supernatural conversation, which will help in "picturing" the spiritual perception that could appear like an abstract concept at this present time.

So what is the Being of Humanity?

First of all from a spiritual perspective, humanity is the physical body of our higher self, the one that is connected to other greater bodies in this universe, which simultaneously communicate with our multidimensional universe. Billions of humans are now on earth, revealing the body of humanity, which is not only spiritual, but also material. We are now seven billions on earth (a figure that keeps increasing a little bit more as I speak), an expansion that is proof that we are becoming a greater organism. As everything is interconnected in the universe, we are therefore wired to each other and to everything, even though this connection is at the moment partially experienced on an unconscious level. We haven't yet come to realize that we are part of a bigger structure, because we are still behaving from the belief of separateness. Every human is bound to come to awareness that he is an individual expression of the whole, living this collective experience from a larger organic structure. Once we become insightful, this realization will transcend the current reality of our small self into the reality of our higher self, which will correlate our personal and collective experiences into one new paradigm. This will be the awakening of the being of humanity, which lies within us.

This being is the timeless and unconditional loving part of ourselves, a spark of the soul, fully conscious of itself. It can only thrive in the physical realm through the reality of our higher self. Only when we have totally embodied our higher self, we will engage in this magnificent cosmic interaction, able to co-exist with other spiritual presences for the benefit of our soul's purpose: transcending the self with love energy, in order to integrate the realm of the soul, where pertains our inner being.

Many "supernatural" beings came upon the earth plane. They incarnated as men or women, and those incarnations from ascended masters still continue now more than ever. One in particular had succeeded to touch the collective heart and mind of our humanity, and still does. His earthly name was Jesus. This being was incarnated as a human being in order to connect us with Christ's consciousness. He came from the soul's realm to demonstrate to us what we are really made of. He broke the nut shell and gave us the seed. He has defined our purpose with this universe. The message was clear: we are here to love ourselves, to forgive our past actions which cannot be changed. We have to learn to let go of our experienced vibrations, so we do not feel influenced by the organic memory, generated by the brain. This memory is a temporary perception of the small self, which restricts the contact with the spiritual reality already contained in this physical body, and which is mostly undermined by the ego mind, due to its lack of consciousness and its fearful state. We are the ones who create this reality, and this reality is revealing who we are through consciousness. To become more conscious means to become more mindful, to become mindful is to tune in to the present moment. The present time is this realm of timelessness, it is where love frequency vibrates fully, and it is where our higher self pertains.

Christ has shown us through his death experience on Earth, that we must transcend our small self: He died on the cross – My interpretation is that the cross represents the four dimensions of this physical plane embodied by the small self. In quantum physics terms, the fourth dimension involves length, width, depth and time. The fifth dimension is related to the "future" beyond the concept of time as we know it in the first three dimensions. The fifth dimension is the reality of the heart. In quantum physics, the fifth and the sixth dimensions link us to infinite possibilities of one future, but this future outcome can only happen through choice. The center of the cross is where the heart of Christ lies. This shows the heart chakra, or as Buddha called it: the middle way, it is the physical plane of love, and the only one that can handle this reality, is the higher self.

The analogy of the cross is showing that, by remaining unconscious through the influence of fear, we became stuck in the realms of the third and fourth dimension. This implies that we must bring consciousness into our minds, in order to realize that we have to love ourselves per se in order to love our minds. Only once we've learned to care for our mind - meaning that we have "to pay attention" to our thinking pattern, to choose our thoughts carefully, as we do the same for our physical body - we wouldn't eat or drink anything that is life threatening for the organism. Once we start to become insightful on an everyday basis, we will be able to understand ourselves and others with minimal resistance from the ego mind. We won't have to get carried away by the loop of our past actions, which make us live in suffering and permanent frustration, and limit our potential to live a greater and kinder reality.

So to reach the reality of the heart, in order to live in the fifth dimension, we have many choices to make. These choices are made consciously or unconsciously. In spiritual terms unconscious choices are made from fearful vibrations, and conscious choices are made from the vibrations of love. Actual conscious choices are made through clarity. Clarity is the most important component in free will. It is the obvious choice that stands out from any other possibilities – so can we call that a choice? Not really, as it is called a pathway. Clarity is conscious free will.

Our choices are what we call free will. Unconscious free will takes you to co-dependency and will always create karmic bonds or, if you prefer to call it, fate. Conscious free will takes you to co-creation and freedom. Conscious free will takes us to the reality of the heart, shifting the focus of our mind from brain to heart. In this situation we no longer use the brain as the only tool for the mind to focus.

The heart also becomes a main organic device for our perceptions - in order to embody our higher self, these two organs must start to work in synchronicity.

This is called in spiritual terms: the ascending process. This is the awakening of the spirit in the mind.

In order to ascend into our higher self: the fifth dimensional body, ascended beings have come here to demonstrate the power of conscious free will, in order for us to perform with that purpose and coordinate the human's mind in this wider organism: the body of humanity. It is a similar process to the cells of our organic body, working together in harmony to constitute one entity. This awakening to conscious free will bring coherent relationships between ourselves and other beings, which are ready to co-create with us on earth and on other planes of existence too. These new harmonized relationships will be highly beneficial for the Earth and the whole universe, as it unifies many organisms with the primary connective energy in the universe: Love.

CHAPTER 2

THE SMALL SELF

"The ego says: once everything falls into place I will feel peace. The spirit says: find your peace and then everything will fall into place"
- Marianne Williamson, spiritual teacher, author and lecturer (born in 1952)

The small self is the little me, the one who had identified with the feeling of separation. When the spirit lives in a reality based on separateness, it starts to create belief systems depending on fear. The small self has a needy attitude toward life, which forces it to always enquire the external world. This seeking attitude creates an extreme frustration within the person, building up more fearful vibrations in the mind and the body. The small self is most of the time unaware of its potential to connect with the universe. Its poor body and mind relationship produces a feeling of emptiness. Its own self becomes a lonely place within, taking us to look without instead of within, and then launches the anxious idea of being forgotten or ignored by others. From this emotional dis-ease a process of self-protection arises, empowering the identified part of this life experience: The ego.

The ego will try everything possible to ensure that it won't be ignored or forgotten, by learning every trick necessary to attract permanent attention. The small self is easily conditioned, as it constantly seeks outside of itself, gradually restricting its inner connection with the universe and mainly with the creative source energy: Love. The ego mind forgets that it is part of the whole, and therefore forgets that it is already loved unconditionally. As we know now this universe is made of energy, and this energy expands into matter naturally, but the small self will strive all its life to cast itself aside from this expansion, believing that this is something happening outside its own mind and body. The small self and the ego are both influenced by the body clock. They are part of the material structure, which obviously lives within a limited time and space reality, due to the transient nature of matter. Therefore, the quest for finding "good" feelings and a safe environment become the dominant motivation and goals of our lower self. This way of thinking can make us live in a delusional world.

Nothing can be changed on the physical plane without the means of creative inner perceptions. The mind is the one who needs to transcend by connecting to the spirit in order to raise its frequency. We must let consciousness penetrate the psyche and transcend it, so we can minimize the mental work, and facilitate the channeling of our higher self.

CHAPTER 3

—◦◦◦◦◦◦◦—

THE HIGHER SELF

*"What you love is a sign from your higher self
of what you are to do"*
> \- Sanaya Roman, Spiritual and
> metaphysic author and teacher.

Our physical body is already complete, and it is built to fulfill the soul's purpose, the active being. Our body is an organic vehicle hosting the individual part of the spirit, in order to bring forth more consciousness into the mind.

The higher self is the greater perspective of ourselves, therefore it is wider and contains much more information and universal connection. It is not only connected to our material realm, but to the mental and spiritual one too. It also houses much more love energy and, consequently, the feeling of insecurity is not present, but we can still feel frustrated at times when we connect to this earthly reality.

This body of humanity is us, without the limitation of the small self. It is the greater connection, the universal communication. We are like an individual cell thriving in this greater body.

We are here to evolve into this humanity, in order to create a powerful organism, connected to the Earth and the cosmos. Greater communication to other intelligences can only be made through the being and body of humanity. By becoming our higher self, we will create this powerful synergy, enabling us to automatically generate more vigorous vibrations and to expend through dimensions.

The humanity's body must be filled with positive energy in order to evolve for the best. It is time to create harmonized environments, well-being and coordination between beings, which will enable us to tap into our greater potential and to acknowledge other types of universal communication. We are a growing humanity through the polarity of the universe contrasting our experience... Yet if we do not embody our higher self, we will become a humanity filled with insecurities and fears. We could develop a limited communication between beings and ourselves, sucking constantly love energy from the environment and other life forms, instead of channeling our own. We could generate more wars and conflicts, just if those around us don't dare to support our endeavors. We could become a cosmic parasite, instead of a creative and cooperative one, thriving to support other earthly and cosmic beings in their expansions.

Therefore, the importance to grow into our higher self is now vital! This is if we do not want to become a cosmic dysfunctional body, living in unconsciousness, which could easily be controlled by fearful, dark entities.

The being of humanity and the higher self are in an interactive and conscious relationship.

Everything and everyone has a higher self and a small self. The higher self is the greater part of the self, because of its larger connection with earthly beings and the universe. We live in an amazing world, but its perception is narrowed down by living life through the small self. Nevertheless the transcendence from the small self into the higher self is not an easy task for the being, especially in our modern societies where everything is related to competition and egoistic thinking. This keeps us focusing on material matter and people's perception. Those demands produce a lot of mental activities, which does require from the body a great amount of energy. The ego will never be satisfied, and so will always be asking for more things to fulfill it. It's like trying to fill with sand a bag which has got a hole at the bottom, and hoping that one day it is going to be filled up... So for the sake of the ego's queries, our societies bring us more and more things to collect and purchase, making this delusional endeavor our reality.

Quantum physics explains that particles will go where ever the observer focuses on, so the reality of the small self becomes denser and denser, and therefore becomes more and more believable for the ego. Although, deep inside of us we can feel that there is another way to be. We can sense that there is a brighter and more loving life to live on earth. This part of us is craving this loving reality, and this side of us is our higher self. It is the part of ourselves that never gives up, regardless the amount of obstacles created and believed by the ego. This side of our selves keeps on dreaming and loving for a more pertinent reality. That is why we are more than just a set of belief systems; we are more than our minds...

We are SPIRITUAL LIVING BEINGS, and our bodies are our energetic shells!

CHAPTER 4

THE SELF AND THE FOCUS

"To conquer frustration, one must remain intensely focus on the outcome, not the obstacles"
- T.F Hodge, writer, blogger,
graphic designer (born in 1969)

The self is multi-dimensional going from low vibrations to high vibrations, also called small self to higher self. It is the energetic scale going from fear to love. We can choose to focus on anything from small to big things, but the energy that enables us to experience this perception will be either from fear or from love.

The focus is accomplished through loving or fearful energy, and which then derives feelings and emotions from these two fundamental powers.

So let's take the example that you want to meet your life partner, but you are feeling insecure or unloved at the moment of focus, and as we know the law of attraction brings you whatever you focus onto, this means that the most dominant vibration in your mind will influence the focus and, thereby, you will attract what comes with this vibration. So you will attract this new relationship, but with the need to release these negative emotions. You will unconsciously target men or women that can bring you this comfort. This can be people with little self-esteem, occupations or interests, meaning they will have plenty of time to give you their attentions. For someone insecure, the idea of being with people who have a busy life style or strong life energy creates too much emotional grief. The focus is a relationship, but the accomplishment of this focus is driven by the energy of fear and lack, which brings you a relationship with all its components such as conditional love, jealousy, inconsideration, ignorance and so on…

This will keep you in the small self, while worrying about the future, instead of developing your life, with awareness and connection. This can only bring you small and short relationships, meaningless situations or experiences, as no one wants to live with the small self for a long time, due to its needy and jealous tendencies.

On the contrary, if you are focusing on a serious romantic relationship with love energy and the feeling of self-worth and appreciation, you are likely to find a long-term partner having a busy and interesting life, but who will have the positive qualities such as: consideration, knowledge, understanding, and compassion. A partner who knows how to take time to do things and discuss matters when required. All loving qualities bring the feeling of contentment, because even if the person is actually busy you can still feel secure, due to good communication skills and acquaintance between the two of you. In loving relationships there is a kindness and calmness that empower the deeds.

Love makes you do things you desire, fear limits you to do only the things you need.

So this analogy explains the difference between focus and experiencing this focus.

The self knows if you are living this life experience from the energy of love or from the apathy of fear, and that's why it is important to know thy self! And mainly to love thyself! Given that it is your direct connection with your inner being and dreams in this physical plane.

Chapter 5

———〰◦◦ᢒᢣ◦◦ᢒᢣ◦◦〰———

The self and energy

"Everything we hear is an opinion, not a fact.
Everything we see is a perspective, not the truth"
- Markus Aurelius, Roman Emperor
and Philosopher (121 -180 AD)

By definition energy is the capacity for work or vigorous power.

This vigorous power enables us to move and materialize this cosmic body which is part of our being.

The self is the connection between the spirit and the soul, and this very precise connection is what we call the universe. Within it emerge all its perspectives, also called dimensions or realities.

The self is therefore what we call the universe, this energetic structure which connects the soul to the spirit.

The soul plane is where our inner being pertains. The self is its envelope and the spirit could be defined as the energetic emanation of the self, whereby a momentum is generated by the spirit and the intense focus from the self which creates a physical body. Space comes from the relationship with the material, physical bodies and the soul plane. The spirit cannot last long in the material world as the intense "gravity" of the self pulls it out. That is why matter is always renewed in order for the spirit to achieve the focus. This can take lives, or let's say many bodies, before a purpose can be fulfilled by one self. The self is the by-product of the soul, and the soul is the body of "love" even though this word can barely describe this mighty power.

What I call mighty power is this acute force that can assemble particles together, creating a structure or body able to communicate with its own self through the spirit.

In essence, this communication is consciousness.

From consciousness another by-product emanates: **the mind**. This takes us to the world of physicality.

Quantum physics explains that there are particles in the universe. These are the tiniest spec of matter that have been observed by human beings so far. By spiritual definition those particles are like "soul dust" which can be transformed and conducted into wavelengths through time and space, following the original vibrations of the universe. The focus of the self has influenced these particles, creating a whole universe and organisms. From the human's scale, those particles interact throughout our own individual part of the self: our spirit, so we also influence those particles, creating our physical reality through our own mind's power and focus.

Chapter 6

———∿∿૦ᄋᐒᐒᐒᐒᐒ૦∿∿———

What is the mind?

*"When we turn the mind inward, god manifest
as the inner consciousness"*
- Ramana Maharshi, Indian
Teacher/guru (1879-1950)

The mind is the unassembled particles, or
the non-materialized part of this focus. The
universe is, as I have described earlier, the
connection between the soul plane and the
self. Therefore, our material body is pure
consciousness assembled. Our bodies are the
vehicles of this purpose. We are there to realize
this purpose, that's why we all have a sense of
mission or realization within. As soon as we
become more conscious the sense of purpose
starts to rise inside us, with this deep knowing

vibrating within our cells. All our physiology is built around this spiritual awareness resonating in the microcosm and macrocosm of the self. So our bodies are a direct link to our soul's purpose, as Jesus Christ stated *"Look for God's Kingdom within"* as there is no other place to be.

As Christ said: *"I am in the father"*

We are now experiencing the mind with this body. We are the individual perspective of the whole.

The mind is itself the by-product of consciousness; it has a very close relationship with matter and is part of all materialization, as physicality is concretization of the mind.

Indeed the mind and the body are the full incarnated aspects of consciousness. Everything in the universe is mind and body, male and female, positive and negative. Consciousness assembled or not yet assembled. That is where the dilemma comes from, where the origin of this fundamental feeling of separateness arises. It is the simultaneous sensation in the spirit of the unassembled and the assembled parts of the mind anchored in physical bodies. These are what create the polarity, the division of the universe.

Love fuses the body and mind into the spirit.

Everything that is not materialized through you will become your environment… "The outside world". For instance, if you are born as a woman, you will experience the environment, this universe, as the masculine, and vice versa. The individual part of us is the whole self incarnated into one of its perspectives. So we will always be the opposite of what we haven't embodied, and what is not embodied by us will always be experienced as its contrast. Only love, the ultimate creative energy, brings equilibrium to this universal paradox.

MIND AND THOUGHTS

*"Between stimulus and response there is a space.
In that space there is the power to choose our
response. In our response lie our growth and our
freedom"*

- Victor. E. Franki, Neurologist
and Psychiatrist (1905-1997)

The mind is the original source for all thoughts.
These thoughts are captured by organic devices.
In the case of cerebral beings, such as human
beings, thoughts are channeled by the brain.
This process is called mental activities. Whilst
the mental activity can differ according to the
individual's intellect, the thinking process and
choice of thoughts is managed by the mind.
The mind is guided by the spirit, and identified

by the ego once the mental process is at work. Thinking is primarily a spiritual process, becoming a mental one once it reaches the material plane.

Science has discovered that the brain does have what it has called neuroplasticity. This means that it is possible to increase the brain functions by changing is neural pathway. When you change your neural pathway, you change the way you think. Consequently you change your reality, as the thoughts you think determine your reality. If you think constructive high vibrational thoughts, you will be living in a high vibrational inner reality, even though the rest of the environment appears to be unbalanced. The same applies to lower vibrational thoughts. The mind is vibrational because it is trapped between the physical plane and the spiritual plane, physicality produced time and space, due to its transient nature, as I mentioned earlier. The spirit never stays too long materialized because of the powerful gravity of the whole self. Matter is not "strong" enough to maintain the soul's focus. In order for the soul to carry out its purpose until achieving total realization, it creates another physical body, in what we call reincarnation. One life experience after another, the spirit carries the unfulfilled purpose. It is unfulfilled due to the fact the spirit became trapped into low vibrational thinking and attachment. Therefore it spends most of its life span in the reality of the small self. This is the job of the spirit to raise the vibrations of its mind, and to transcend the small self so it can spend its time in the reality of the higher self.

This is why the importance of thinking bright thoughts is so important! Many spiritual practices offer some mental tools, to assist the mind with the process of non-identification. If we can start living our lives from our higher self and serve its purpose, then we will be able to transcend the mind with the energy of love. We can become a whole being again.

For instance, a lot of people have described Jesus as a being of light and, in the book of revelation, it is written that Jesus was a being of pure loving light. Christ says *"I am the Alpha and the Omega"*- Alpha meaning the beginning and Omega meaning the end.

"I am the beginning and the end". Once we have become this being of light again we are ending the karmic circle on the physical plane. We do not need to reincarnate anymore, as we have fulfilled the purpose, this part of the self has become whole again.

We only feel separated from the ego perspective, as the ego is the mental identification to this physical structure and the by-product of emotional and physical life experiences. But this can be reversed and changed. Obviously this sounds easier said than done… As it is actually a challenge to undo our conditioning from our ego mind. The illusion of the ego is so powerful, that a part of us has totally identified with its perspective, especially when supported by the collectiveness.

We must acknowledge that we are temporarily divided but eternally connected. We are one spiritual being craving to co-create in this transient universe. It is our collective quest.

CHAPTER 8

⸺⧫⸺

BEING OF HUMANITY AND MATTER

"Science cannot solve the ultimate mystery of nature. And that is because, in the last analyses, we ourselves are the past of this mystery that we are trying to solve"
- Max Planck, Theoretical Physicist and Nobel prize in physic in 1918 (1858-1947)

The being of humanity can start to reveal itself, as we gradually gain more and more consciousness, which will create a direct relationship between spirit and matter, managed by our high vibrational mind.

It is true that the physical body feels separated by the senses, and it is actually part of a greater organism in the universe. This larger body is the body of humanity, but it is simply "asleep". This means it is living most of the time de-synchronized with the rest of the world, ignorant of the multi-dimensional reality of its being. It is a matter of "waking it up" by reconnecting to our spiritual mind and start thinking consciously. We must attract trusting thoughts in order to reach the spirit, and let it "drive" our bodies. Everything is interconnected, as we are the same being within different levels of existence. Once we have acknowledged our multi-dimensional structure, then we will start to re-coordinate with the rest of what we are: The self.

Nothing stays still in the universe, everything is dynamical and interconnected because the universe is the connection between the soul's plane and the self, with this connection producing what we call energy. This energy creates matter.

CHAPTER 9

---∿∽◦◦◦◦◦◦◦◦∿---

BEING OF HUMANITY AND THE BRAIN

"The only reason for time is so that everything doesn't happen at once"
> - Albert Einstein, Theoretical physicist (1879-1955)

So is there only present time? Well yes… in reality there is only now! But the small self lives in the illusion of the mind caught into memory. The memory is actually a storage space in the brain, which records all the information necessary for the survival of the being. The brain keeps the being alive by creating a well-known reality, which will make the reality predictable, a sort of comfort zone maintained by the brain activity; therefore we can function unconsciously and interact between each other without needing to renew our thoughts or physical skills. This attitude from the brain is needed for the maintenance of the organic structure. This task is paramount for the brain, as it also depends on it.

The spiritual realm is not something that the brain can yet completely comprehend, due to its primary function based on survival. As our societies became less and less physically dangerous, the brain started to relax, allowing spiritual matter to be gradually acknowledged. Nevertheless there is still a strong identity and traumas from the past retained in the lower self, and its vibrational state is inhibiting the greater reality of our higher self.

The brain is a thought receptor. It is what processes information through the nervous system. Those data are first sensed by the heart, and then the brain reacts accordingly.

That's where the sensation of an outer and inner world come from, as anatomically there is indeed a nervous circuit created for the "outer" environment felt by the heart, equipped with the five senses, and which trigger the sensory neurons and create a reaction from our "inner" environment. This task is managed by the brain via the motor neurons. So yes indeed, we can understand why we have the sensation of being separated from the rest of the world. But if we base our thinking on a higher plane, the spiritual plane, then we can realize that the "outer" world is simply the non-focus part of our being. Relatively, the inner world is our temporary identity, our person, our own single piece of the whole.

The brain is capable of flexibility, but it is also very selective. It has a filter called the reticular active system (RAS) which filtrates information. This triage is performed according to our interpretation and beliefs of "what we think is real and what we think is not".

For example, if you think that being wealthy is not possible for you, then your brain will validate this belief by excluding any thoughts related to a wealthy reality. This is pure neuro-linguistic programming, as the brain can only serve the reality according to our beliefs. Our brains are there to serve us, and if we say this is my reality, then be it for the brain. It will do everything to ensure that we get what we want, as it believes us, and follows us, obviously because without us it cannot exist. This is why it is so important to choose belief systems that bring joy and fulfillments to our lives, in order for our brains to work for our best interests.

Chapter 10

BEING OF HUMANITY AND THE HEART

"The Heart has its reasons, which the reason knows not"
- Blaise Pascal, French mathematician, physicist, inventor and philosopher (1623-1662)

For the physical body the heart is the feelings receptor.

It is the one that connects the physical plane to the spiritual plane, by sensing the vibrations of thoughts. The positive or negative feelings felt by the heart, gives an idea of the spiritual environment: the scale goes from love to fear, what the brain defines as positive or negative thinking. Our thoughts are the product of these feelings, and the brain arranges them according to our memory and set of beliefs.

The heart seems to be the only organ really living in the now!

As it is also the first organ created in the embryo (after about five weeks). There is discrepancy between the present moment and the acknowledgement of the spiritual environment by the brain. The present moment, or call it our spiritual connection, is already obsolete by the time it reaches the brain. The brain is slower than the heart, as it has more complex work to do, but mainly it can be limited by the mental activity, which can then affect the other organs.

Regarding our heart, it is more than just a pump. It is the one that tells you where your spirit is standing in this universe. The heart is a physical and spiritual device for the body. It could be described as the "mystic organ" the gateway for the spirit onto the physical plane.

"The heart is the door to the soul, as the eyes (the brain) are the window to the soul."

Let's analyze this for a moment:

The heart is the door to the soul, a good metaphor is: open your heart, or living life with an open heart.

Regarding the brain, we say: the eyes are the window of the soul. This could mean that the spirit enters the organic body from the heart and settles in the brain area, using the "eyes" and other senses to experience physicality. But this is only if we let our spirit do its job, although *"deep inside our heart"* we know that we are nothing less than our spirit. This tendency we have developed with time, and many relationships with others have made us identify with our so-called "personality" this person is actually the by-product of our autonomic thinking pattern designed by the brain functions from the moment we were born. We are, therefore, not really "awake" spiritually speaking, because we are living unconsciously most of the time, manipulated by a "reality template" made up by our memory which purely exists to protect the body. This memory is also supported by a bigger template: the collective reality, and in a collective way it is called history.

Our history is retracing the collective memory. This collective reality is supported by testimonies collected throughout the years, based on an educational system, and which has been created to ensure that we will convey this thinking pattern in order to carry on the work of our ancestors. This puts our brains at peace, but in the meantime slows down our spiritual progress, due to its tendency to be just there living according to "social status". Meanwhile, the logic part of the mind is there to cope with the laws of the universe, and different activities of daily living, through which is created our own human's rules too: I like to call it *"the rules of human behavior"* - rules which are like a social language, dictated by a government, in order to maintain certain behaviors toward each other, as the prime part of our human nature isn't totally controlled by most of us, and will never be if we live life from the ego mind. So, by trying to cope with laws and codes of conduct, we have developed another mode of behavior inside of us, the egoistic mode, and this is the most fearful part of our selves, conditioned and maintained for the well-being of this social enterprise. The ego is the identification to this limited reality, and it is the essence of our personality. The ego will do anything to keep this body alive, in the best way, and is there to defend and serve its creator: The brain.

So the reality of the heart has been taken over by the reality of the brain, it is ego versus spirit, past versus present. Although, the spirit doesn't fight the ego but instead tries to transcend it into its alter ego.

The heart is the organ living in the present moment, the bridge between the here and the now. In our heart lies our presence.

CHAPTER 11

———~~⌒⌒⌒⌒~~———

ROOT BELIEF

"It takes a very long time to become young"
                    - Pablo Picasso, Spanish artist-
                                painter (1881-1973)

Why is it so important for human beings to cultivate innocence?

Because by doing so you are creating a bond with spirit and mind, restricting the construction of the ego mind.

But instead we have created societies based on the egoistic part of ourselves, directing our children toward the small self, by intellectualizing everything and implementing knowledge that are not stimulating our spiritual mind. We are asked to perform when young, when the time for playfulness and environmental bondage is still necessary.

This stops the mind growing with the spirit, creating a dis-ease, a mental discomfort, which later in life could develop into mental disorders, creating all sorts of vices and destructive behaviors within our being. Locking our spirits in the small self, it will settle down with the vibrations of fear. This unhealthy environment can cause the being to develop a great obsession with death, due to lack of self-love and spiritual bondage.

For instance, all child abuse is a spiritual trauma; the more terrible the abuse is the more the person is likely to live in fear, making it self-centered and destructive, due to the intense mental activity between the spirit and the ego. This bipolar activity happens mostly at the subconscious level, showing up some times at the conscious level when triggered by a memory or a similar action. Any abuse in childhood or in adulthood creates a shock for the brain and for the rest of the body, leaving a blueprint of this memory in the neurological system. In a way we can say that this shockwave nails the being to a low vibrational plane. It will take a great deal for the spirit to erase this blueprint, as a neural pathway would have been created almost instantly in the brain, affecting the mind process. When one positive or negative event happens during childhood, then this becomes the thinking "center of gravity", the root belief of the spirit for a lifetime, or more.

Each plane has its "gravity" or center of attraction and the human's plane has got one too. But the faculty for human beings to think consciously can be acquired and this can change our root beliefs, our center of attraction. Becoming conscious is to awaken to what we really are, and not letting our past dictate our life experiences. It is hard for the spirit to transcend the ego after a strong charge of negative energy, especially when it happened during childhood, as the brain will be "modeled" around this root belief. So when a certain experience persists in your life, it is vital to understand the origin of this attraction, to find out the root belief that makes you live this experience over and over again. Once you have found out the belief that limits your expansion, it will become easier to transform it to your greater advantage.

In bringing clarity and relief to the mind, events will unfold more naturally until you can take full charge of your life's purpose again.

CHAPTER 12

————— ∽∾⌒⊶⊷⌒∾∽ —————

PHYSICALITY AND
THE SPIRIT

"What we are is God's gift to you, what you become is your gift to God"
- Hans Urs Von Balthasar, Swiss Theologian
and catholic priest (1905-1988)

The universe is bipolar and therefore has physicality too, the body lives between pleasure and pain, and the same applies for the mind fluctuating from the state of joy and suffering.

This gives more opportunity for the ego to get trapped in one plane or the other. The spirit is really challenged in the physical plane due to these paradoxes, but the purpose cannot be stopped. The spirit is aware of all those obstacles, and its aim is to get through them with maximum consciousness (maximum insight between the soul and the self), and to transcend its mind with love. All those experiences, life time after life time, have brought density to the spirit, but it has to get lighter in order to raise the vibration of its mind. Lighter means to become more and more conscious, more present, to gradually decrease the amount of mental activity. This can be achieved by not mentally identifying to the action, but by just living the experience of those acts.

Experience is like a tool used to extract the knowledge from the action.

By experiencing life, we extract its knowledge, its juice out of the actions. The experience permits the being to become aware of its environment and to develop its talents, enabling accuracy and insight. It gradually frees the spirit from mental activities in the physical body, and raises the vibration of the mind. In contrast, identification gets us trapped in the law of cause and effect or, as it is called in Indian terms, the Karma. Although once we start allowing, instead of identifying, the spirit is able to learn with minimal involvement in the consequences. There is no need to understand why this had happened or what would have been if... because the law of cause and effect has an infinity of probabilities.

We can learn from life and its struggles, instead of spending our time fixing them. And it is by itself the ultimate probability, as this learning will automatically bring clarity and consciousness into the mind, and increase its vibrations. The allowing process will give us more creative energy, which will naturally integrate the mind; to reconnect us to the ultimate reality, as in fact there is only one self and spirit all connected by love. Oneness is the ultimate reality, and this reality is experienced through love. When we are not consciously living in love, we believe in fear as fear is the belief of being separated from love. This illusion is very strong in the universe and countless beings, including us, are trapped into it.

But this is also speaking and living life from the perspective of the lower self.

We are indeed "separated" from the point of view of purpose, as each being must fulfill a part of it, using its own talent. We are the universe, and the separation appears real only when we are focusing on the universal paradoxes. Yes, matter does bring spiritual division, but only if we are living each experience through the ego perspective, and if we are emotionally attaching ourselves to it.

When we regain consciousness, we can see that what the ego interprets as separation is actually a state of being.

We have to let the spirit be and feel with the body in order to access more consciousness and transcend its reality.

CHAPTER 13

―――ᶸᵐᵒᵒᶜᵉᵒᵒᵉᵒᵒ――――

HIGHER SELF AND THE SPIRITUAL PURPOSE

"Your purpose in life is to find your purpose and to give your whole heart and soul to it"
- Gautama Buddha, Sage Siddhartha
Gautama (born in 623 BC)

So what is the purpose?

The purpose is to transcend the universal mind with love, to make it whole again, by being totally connected to one's self. Once the mind loves itself, then the spirit can feel fulfilled and complete again, breaking the pattern of dual thinking, it will match the vibrations of the soul's realm, and will transcend the whole universe into it, freeing our inner beings from this material experience.

The spirit is a mediator between matter and soul, it is the one that can acknowledge love and bring it forth in the materialized part of the mind.

Love is the most powerful energy, and it emanates from the soul plane.

Love is a connective energy which creates matter by the power of focus, but matter evolves and expands, due to the constant creation of love.

Love is a permanent creation, but this state creates a sense of polarity into the mind. This feeling of duality comes from the constant transcendence of physicality within a mind which has got a limited amount of consciousness.

Consciousness is pure awareness of the spirit - whatever you are conscious of, define it as reality. In fact reality is revealed by consciousness. Consequently your reality is what you are conscious of. So we can say that reality is a mind state, as consciousness takes place in the mind in order for the body to experience it.

The being is always conscious, but the lack of mindfulness within this life experience traps the mind into a repetitive thought pattern, this forces us to live in our sub-reality, the one created by the subconscious mind. Once we are awakened to our spiritual path, we can then see our reality shaping around our goals and purpose. We are gradually adjusting our mind and body to the Epi-reality, the one that we are conscious of, diminishing progressively the sub-reality.

The more awareness we gain, the more we expand and renew our reality.

We bear this feeling of separation only because we are conscious of a small part of the universe, a small part of us. By increasing our consciousness, we expand our reality, we become gradually whole again. We are able to feel and be with the energy of love.

The feeling of separateness is only increasing the vibration of fear. The delusional thinking of the ego can keep the spirit trapped into ignorance and limiting beliefs.

The way to add more consciousness within our minds is to regain faith in the whole creation process. The fact that we live and identify to this conditioning makes it hard, or almost impossible, to regain total faith in ourselves. But for this, we need to go beyond the concept of believing we have to be and live only for our dreams, in order to become faithful to them. Only then we will understand that our dreams are actually our "Epi-reality" (epi has the meaning of above), where lies our awareness. Dreams are the essence of our purpose. Once we start to acknowledge that, faith will naturally take place in our heart, transferring us from the reality of our lower self to the one of our higher self in this present lifetime.

Faith is beyond belief, as believing is a mental state. Faith is the spiritual knowing, the connection with the power that generates love.

This power is what we are really made of. It is the source of life.

Our inner being is one individual "perspective" of this power, one "expression" of the source.

The self connects to the mind through the spirit, but at this stage it will really depend on the person's spiritual growth (the independent part of the material experience) through life experiences.

The spirit may live life through the small self, and get trapped in fear and mental limitations, until it grows from a believer mind state to a faithful being. Only the higher self can expand constructively in this reality. To be our higher self, we have to live in the now, we have to become conscious of the present moment, because the present time is the "Epi-reality" the reality of the heart. When we feel connected to the greater part of ourselves, we simply feel our spirits experiencing this time-space reality through our higher self. Then once we have become the higher self, we will automatically transcend this time-space reality into "time limitless" reality, which will outstrip our ego mind too.

The consciousness of the higher self is so big that it is aware of the universal duality without being affected by it, because it has a conscious relationship with the whole self and its spirit. It is soulful.

Living through our higher self will enable us to gain great influence on the universe. We will live by the universal laws without feeling ruled by them. We will use the laws without having to dread them, as we will understand that these universal laws are here to serve the purpose of one's self. They are the byproduct of the mechanical process of the soul working through matter.

In this new paradigm we will live our lives for the purpose, by practicing our talents for the benefit of humanity, nourishing our collective mind with our spiritual awareness.

We will work together with one mind, through the expression of our individual talent. This harmonious interaction between each other will shape our societies and environment, creating a new form of communication between beings.

This high vibrational world will reveal other realms, and beings within these dimensions will feel inspired to contact us for the purpose of universal co-creation. Angels and ascended Masters will broadcast their visions and teaching straight to our collective mind, filling our minds with love and creative energies on a daily basis. It will be like attuning our minds to the frequencies of Heaven.

CHAPTER 14

MIND AND BODY

*"To keep the body in good health is a duty…
Otherwise we should not be able to keep our
mind strong and clear"*
- Gautama Buddha, Sage Siddhartha
Gautama (born in 623 BC)

The mind is what we call reality, we live according to what we think, and therefore our reality is made of thoughts. We cannot stop thinking in this body, as we are made of thoughts.

Let me explain, we come forth to express a primary desire from the soul.

The soul's desire is to fill the mind with love.

Our intuitions are our heart expressing this fundamental desire in our physical conditioning. Love is by itself pure communication; this expression is what creates coherence in the universe. From this expression derives consciousness, and from consciousness derives a vibrational field called: the mind. Matter creates division in the spirit and in the mind which causes the mind to split into what we call thoughts.

Thoughts are pure particles of this manifestation.

The thoughts are then channeled by organic devices, such as the brain in our case. But prior to that, the state of mind is felt by the heart, and then the brain will distribute this information to the rest of the body, which will react accordingly.

Matter is the manifestation of the soul's focus, it is structured with light particles, and these light particles are the energy of love.

Therefore we can say that we are made of light; living through the focus of the soul.

The body is the primary physical manifestation created by love, and then the process can continue on from the body to manifest more matter. Physicality is self-sufficient at first, but needs love to remain structured.

Love only needs to create "once", as we call the original pattern of the universe the primary focus.

But matter can be maintained only with love energy.

If the matter is lacking love energy it will gradually deconstruct itself.

That is where the extreme anguish from the ego comes from. Nevertheless it is natural to dread death, when we stand in the vibration of fear. Fear takes us to destructive behaviors, due to its ignorance of love energy. Matter can deconstruct because of the belief in fear, which is simply ignorance. Physical pain is by itself manifestation of fear energy in the body. It is anxiety of the cells. Fear has got its own onset of feelings, which trigger what we call negative thinking. Nevertheless there is nothing to cure that, except for gaining more awareness. Many human beings try to experience love in many different ways, but it seems that the most powerful and direct to us is the creation of another living being; when a conscious being gives birth to another conscious being, it is like a direct bond with love. This connection becomes permanent in this lifetime, and even if this being comes with a different thoughts pattern and vibrations, they are still connected directly through matter.

Having a child is an intense spiritual experience, as we can feel the spirit as one but knowing that we are in separated bodies. The spirit demonstrates this feeling of oneness through what we call family. When love is anchored into two physical bodies through their genetics, then even matter cannot trick them anymore, fear cannot dominate their thinking pattern. Although sharing our genetics directly in this lifetime does help the ego mind to be permanently reminded of spiritual oneness, it is also possible to experience oneness even if the beings have not been genetically bonded with another. A person such as Mother Theresa, for instance, had this spiritual connection through her faith and love for humanity. This bond with her fellow humans was as strong as a parent for a child.

Matter is organized according to physical laws and universal principles. This configuration operates with the mind. When the mind is interacting with the body, a dynamic is created, and this triggers a permanent exchange between these two aspects of the universe, but the one that is directing the whole process is the spirit.

The spirit is within all the time; it is the presence in the absence of the ego.

In the end everything is spirit, even matter, therefore to try to separate each thing by using names and analogies, helps the mind to grasp the essence of this knowledge.

We need to be this knowledge; in order to live it completely without committing to the ego.

The mind and body relationship is paramount for the spirit to be here. But this relationship must be balanced and vigorous. It should energize the body.

A happy mind makes a healthy body, in contrary to a sick mind poisoning the body with fear and ego attacks. Therefore we consider our body as our spiritual home base. It is the one that houses the spirit for a lifetime, and the mind is its fuel, the one that activates the mechanism in order to create a dynamic between matter and spirit.

For this reason, the mind must be filled with constructive thoughts in order to initiate a coherent dynamism between the body and the environment.

CHAPTER 15

---∿≀≗≀⊙⊱≗⊱≀∾---

EGO AND ALTER EGO

"Part of me suspects that I am a loser and the other part of me thinks that I am a God almighty"
- John Lennon, Musician, song writer and singer for the worldwide famous band The Beatles (1940-1980)

The ego is the part of the spirit which has identified with the body and its life experience.

There is a great amount of control in the ego, as it is seeking physical comfort in order to limit the spiritual experience when identifying with the small self.

The vibrations of the small self create the worst climate for the ego, as its primary role is to identify to this life experience, and mainly to the body. But the reality of the small self brings unsecure thoughts into the mind, and consequently disturbs the body mechanism. This lack of connection with love energy from oneself affects the functionality of the organs, and weakens the body's immune system.

This leads the ego to all sorts of destructive behaviors, toward others and its environment, due to the incoherent relationship with its mind and body. The feeling of separation is provoked by the lack of spiritual experience, as the small self is constantly seeking itself in others, making this situation very daunting for the being. The absence of trust in its external environment will make it over protective towards the body, ready to do anything to keep it alive in the best conditions. The ego mind defends its body like a wild animal facing a danger. Everyday reality is a real challenge, as the ego is constantly seeking attention from others, due to its poor capacity to self-love.

Yet once living from the higher self, the ego will transit to the alter ego, and this will enable the spirit to co-operate actively with kindness and discernment from the dimension of the body-mind. Its identification to the body is also linked to the self, erasing the sense of separateness. The alter ego is the best medium for the spirit in this physical body, it is a faithful companion. Once the ego has changed into the alter ego, it will be capable of sensing the positive and reassuring vibrations, making it relaxed with the process, and be able to start a coherent interaction with the spirit. At its service, it will ensure that the body receives what it needs, in order to be more connected with love energy and more efficient with the spiritual purpose. The alter ego knows that the quicker the job is done, the faster it will return to its original realm, the source of all phenomena and excitement, permanent love. In this context the ego will not fear the environment anymore, but will see it as an amazing opportunity to bring love on earth, to convey Heaven upon Earth. Here is the purpose of all beings.

Although the alter ego can be challenged by the fast living pace of the spirit, and the demanding amount of physical actions, we never lose our ego or alter ego, as it is a natural structure of the spirit under physical conditions. It is the "armor" of the spirit. The identification of the alter ego is important, as it brings focus to the mind, as long as we do not identify to the egotist aspect of our spirit from the small self perspective when living this life experience. The alter ego is there to serve the spirit by bringing focus to the mind. Only then we will experience life through our higher self with minimal fluctuation of our mental state.

Chapter 16

—⁓⦿⟶⟶⦿⟵⟶⦿⟵⟵—

The shift

"A small body of determined spirits fired by an unquenchable faith in their mission can alter the course of history"
- Mahatma Gandhi, Indian nationalist leader for human rights and freedom (1869-1948)

So the time for change has come... the shift is occurring right now! The spirit is penetrating the body with hard strokes, transcending the ego and awakening the mind... What we call the shift is the embodiment of the spirit and its purpose into our body and mind.

This change brings great distress to the ego, due to its main tendency to compare itself to others, as the ego is always seeking for outer reassurance. The ego is comfortable with uniformity, although the change is about bringing the diversity of our unique skills into a unified society. Therefore the ego has to check to see if this is a collective manifestation. The ego will resist the change and try to fight it until the collectiveness demonstrates that it is shifting too. For this to happen collectively, we must start accepting the individual change within. Nothing can be done until we experience this life from our higher self.

The being of humanity can be proactive through the higher self. The higher self makes all of us work in a synchronistic fashion. It brings everyone to the realization of who and what we are, by revealing what we are meant to do for the benefit of all.

We are like cells thriving in an organic body. We are the beings hosted in the body of humanity. In the physical body, each cell works by function and co-operation with each other within a mellifluous way. That is because they are not influenced by the ego mind but directly work within the spiritual realm, gaining force and capacity from the core of the universe, tapping into the primary connective energy of the self: love.

Nowadays, knowing what our talent is, in order to generate a financial income from it, is becoming our main purpose. We are finding hard to agree with spending our energy through an activity which is not in affinity with ourselves. The being of humanity can function only when enough beings have awakened - "When enough cells are activated". The shift is revealing our deepest desires for life, and urges us to work and produce "currency" with our natural talents.

As we are awakening, we are letting go of any resistance from the ego. This process makes us recognize the spiritual presence within us and within everything. Like the organic cells in our physical body, we must follow the cosmic rhythm of our inner being, letting the spirit of this universe direct our mind.

The egotist structure will try its best to avoid this shift. When the ego settled down in the body, it had created its own reality and rules, only to seek more and more comfort and control. However, the shift brings pressure on the organic structure, triggering discomfort and physical pain, due to the strong conditioning of living unconsciously with most of the spiritual aspect of our being. We have practiced "spiritual laziness" for so long, by distracting ourselves with outer events, letting the small self fantasizes on the creations of the universe. The transition is intense, as our entire physical and mental structures have been modeled around this unfit reality. As an analogy we can use the example of someone who has been ill and had to stay in bed for a long period of time. This time of non activity had wasted his muscles away, but, once the patient starts to feel better, a physiotherapist will come to re-educate his mobility. The workout at first will feel like hell for the person, due to intense pain and discomfort applying on the muscles. Rehabilitation requires tremendous physical and mental efforts at first. Actually, the healing process is the most painful of all. Eventually the person can regain muscle strength by constant exercising and coaching, replacing stiffness with flexibility.

Obviously there are many factors contributing to the rehabilitation of an individual, but this is to give an idea of how hard it is for the mind and body to break through certain habits and tendencies, that is why other beings of the spiritual realm must be invocated to come and support this shift. And is also why spirituality in many forms is now blossoming everywhere, and everyone has got a spiritual interest, including scientists, coaches, philosophers, etc… They are all realizing the importance of a holistic program in their methods which include our spiritual aspect too. They start to see that if we do not take care of our multi-dimensional "structure", our survival and development as a being is compromised and limited by the realm of fear, disabling the person and, on a collective scale, creating a dysfunctional society.

Nevertheless the concern for the ego to go through this transformation brings emotional anxiety. The struggles come from the lack of reciprocity from other human beings at first, as everyone awakens at a different pace. We all have felt this calling inside for a long time, and now it has amplified in this lifetime. The outcome of new technology, such as the internet, brings a fresh perspective on human communication and the sharing of information. We are no longer limited by a grouping of mainstream media, but can also receive information from all over the planet and from anyone. We can see that we, too, have the urge to express our feelings and share the reality of our inner being to the world, while people are becoming more and more aware of a greater reality coming upon us. It is becoming undeniable, as this magnificent reality is now revealed by us connecting with each other on an everyday basis within no time and without geographic barriers.

This planet is gradually becoming one home for all of us. The technology of transportation is also getting faster and faster, decreasing time and space. Now more things can be done, more experiences can be lived in one lifetime. This stimulates the spirit to travel around the planet, and therefore meet new people from all around the world, triggering an instant physical contact, which reduces the thinking process and increases our physical fitness. The whole earth feels like one same place, it feels like a big home base. As a consequence, the natural effect of this new way of living is the communion of every human being with this global enlivening, exposing a need for a constant connection with like-minded people, in order to express and develop what we enjoy the most.

Like the cells of our body, we begin to follow a bigger pattern, revealing the design of a larger structure: The body of humanity.

The shift is therefore a collective connection between us, humans, netting the mind with every single string of intelligence that we are. This is designing our communities, like the cells uniting with similar form and function, creating what we call an organ, which serves a specific task for the body. These organs then collaborate with each other, in order to give life to a larger body: the human's body.

Once we have become conscious enough, the dynamic between our mind and the Being of humanity can take place.

We will all awaken one by one, and this awakening will expose us to our talents, the ones that will enable the potent interaction and healthy function of our humanity.

This growth makes us shift from our small self to our higher self. This is implying an enormous degradation of the current paradigm, which is already showing in our everyday news, and the present power at work is progressively struggling to control the spiritual beings that we are becoming. The current governments try to control the Being of humanity through a global order, in order to continue their agenda of manipulation and retention of spiritual information to the population. It is pure propaganda from the collective ego mind. The Being of humanity isn't an order, it is a spiritual development based on benevolence and synchronized interaction with one another. No domination is needed. Once we all become our higher self the feeling of division and competition will be replaced naturally by the feeling of unity and co-operation. That is why the work on self-development is so paramount right now!

We must start to learn to quiet our minds. Many teachers are now out there to help us do the work. It is just a matter of choosing the technique corresponding to our awakening pace and skills. Assistance from the supernatural planes is available to everyone, from every country and culture. It has been translated by the ascended Masters in many different ways, in order for each of us to grasp their knowledge and support.

Soon the contrast between the new paradigm and the old one will appear obvious for all of us. This will boost the process for the ones ready to transcend, but for some others this will appear to be devastating, as some people have achieved everything in their lives from the ego mind, ignoring the deeper part of themselves in order to avoid the spiritual work, due to egotistic addiction of pleasure and comfort, and obviously encouraged by the actual social system, as that is mostly ego mind based too. We have believed in the reality of the small self for so long, and so have our parents and ancestors. Although the ancient world did talked about our greater part. This multi-dimensional being has been described in many ancient texts and art works. They knew already that, something that we have forgotten through material progress and this obsession with wars and conquests. We have become gradually enslaved to our own wickedness.

It is in our genetic, it is part of our history to reinforce the existence of our small self. In the old paradigm it sounds like a mad thing to say that there is something else than us at work too, and to state that some of the things we have lived for are now obsolete or misinterpreted, put a cynical smile on the face of the ego-minded. I must admit that this is a real shock for the mind, suddenly having to think differently, having to acknowledge new thoughts on a daily basis. It was for me and still is. The neurological work appears to be enormous. But this cannot be stopped. This is the natural expansion of the human heart-minded.

CHAPTER 17

A GLIMPSE OF THE
NEW WORLD

*"We are moving away from the negativity of
the old Earth, and it's going to be a complete
turnaround, beyond belief, and we are all going
there now"*
- Dolores Cannon, past life regression
Hypnotherapist, and Author (born in 1931)

Nothing should be feared, because once we
gain trust in this new perception, we will feel
free from the negativity within. We will finally
be able to express our greater skills on a daily
basis, for the good functioning of the humanity.
Nothing will be hidden from us, and this will
bring such a joy to the spirit, as it is part of the
purpose to live in transparence in order to let

the truth shine through our beautiful mind and body. We are meant to work within this cosmic rhythm, to unify the cellular world with the spiritual one, to all engaged with harmonious intentions, for the learning and discovery of our life purpose. Feeling the energy of love spreading in the physical realms, will become the original excitement of living in this new human paradigm, unleashing an immense improvement of our mental state, increasing physical capacities and life span, interacting positively with the environment...this will bond us to its core.

All technology will be at the service of our highest potential, but also for an active contact with other beings; this will create a new form of emotional language between earthly beings and other cosmic creatures. We will use pure communication, tapping directly into loving energies in order to co-create for the well-being of the universe. The egoistic obstacles will be limited by this strong feeling of faith, this feeling of belonging to the whole universe, realizing its influence at the core of our being.

Many people are commencing to awaken to that feeling. We have now more and more demands of spiritual based teaching, techniques and "life style". And this is simply because the process is accelerating via modern technologies. This channeling of radio frequencies in the electromagnetic web is the tool for communicating without physical limits. The potential to connect with each other is now very high; this conducts the information at one given moment to the collectiveness, and in a very short period of time. This can be compared in human physiological anatomy to the central nervous system (CNS). It is an exchange of information, from outside (the environment) to inside (the Being of humanity), in physiological terms this would be the work of the sensory neurons to the motor neurons. This dynamism between cells is essential in order to maintain the body alive and reactive to any negative stimulus.

The Being of humanity is, by itself, a greater organism on planet earth; and once totally awakened it will become a full being able to cooperate with other intelligences, which already have gone through the transformative process. These beings will automatically contact us, once we collectively awaken to our full potential and individual talent.

But for now we are at the transformative stage, growing from embryo (old paradigm) to living being (new paradigm) ready to leave the womb. This birth will be intense, as the fetus stage was challenged by strong negativity. This body has a few maligned cells already, and it is facing eventual destructive consequences. A lot of human beings are contaminated with this dis-ease.

Nothing is lost yet, but the delivery could be very painful for us and which could eventually affect the environment. Some other living beings are also feeling the shift, as this is happening to the whole universe, not forgetting that we are the universal focus and that we are all inter-connected.

So your focus is as important as mine, or other creatures on earth or elsewhere in the cosmos. Once we understand that we are one conscious part of the whole self, we will start to gain consciousness naturally and gradually, although the process will depend on our capacity to adjust to the reality of the higher self, and which will rely on how much we can detach from the lower self.

This shift from lower to higher reality is an individual and global mechanism. Therefore, we must first learn to accept, in order to allow everyone to move toward this new reality at their own time and pace.

It is obviously a hard one, when it comes to accept the pace of our loved ones. As we are so emotionally attached to them, we have the tendency to be more intolerant with people we are close to, simply because deep inside we wish we could do that together, in order for us not to have to face our emotional distress. Unfortunately, this is not always possible, even more so when it comes to spiritual development. This can feel like a very lonely work to do, when perceived from the vision of the lower self, as it is attracting thoughts bound by time and space, therefore making it a slave of its own memory. This inhibits the elevation of the mind, and narrows the channeling of more positive and loving thoughts.

Once the acknowledgement of non-duality is acquired as the ultimate reality in this universe, then we can surrender to the ascending process.

In order to elevate our thoughts, we must drop the ones that keep us attached to a limited belief system, or to a painful memory. We must detoxify our minds and bodies from old energies.

To release those heavy vibrations for good, we must learn to listen to our inner being and forgive our small self. It is also followed by a physical healing process which includes change of diet and body work. Let's say that we are about to enter the recovery period.

CHAPTER 18

FORGIVENESS, THE
BRIDGE BETWEEN THE
OLD PARADIGM AND
THE NEW REALITY

"I am forgiving and releasing this memory from my being, I am moving on by letting the source of Life take care of any effects upon this conscious action"

— Veronique Bianconi, Body worker,
author and artist (born in 1974)

We have got to let love take care of the consequences when we are releasing the energy of fear. It is like letting the whole fabric of the universe "recycle" this negative memory for us. We can serve the purpose, once we implement love energy in the mental process, for the sake of bringing full consciousness to the mind. The spirit must become conscious in order to stop the influence of fear in its thinking process. But before that, the self has to become free from the influence of its polarity, in order to complete the soul's purpose.

To clear away this feeling of separation from its physical embodiment, the self has to love every part of its own creation through the spirit.

For this to happen, each perspective of its own self must be appreciated and acknowledged by the spirit. And acknowledgement comes naturally after the process of forgiveness, as the mental resistance drop off, revealing the learning of this experience.

Forgiving doesn't mean that we are not taking responsibility for our own actions. However, instead of trying to control these personal events, we ask the source to assist us by enhancing this life experience with more understanding. We must trust the natural mechanism and let go, discharging the person from managing those emotions intellectually. Thereby, we can start to use our intellectual potential in the service of constructive and meaningful tasks. The process of forgiveness is also helping the brain to save more energy, which will enhance physical life energy and well-being in the body. The brain is the organ that burns the most calories, due to its intense mental workout. The thinking process demands an extra amount of energy to be consumed and fatigue the brain, leaving less energy for the rest of the organs, and bringing stress to the metabolism.

Therefore, we can say that faith and forgiveness are comparable to the subconscious work, which in physiological terms is called the autonomic nervous system (ANS). For example the respiratory system or the digestive system is controlled by the autonomic nervous system, we do not need to remind our lungs to breathe, we do not need to ask our gastro intestinal track to dissolve and convert the different substances in our body every time we eat or drink something. So the same could apply to our spiritual work, letting some emotions be taken care of by the source of life, so we do not have to invest ourselves in the analyses of some events that do not serve us and destroy us gradually, too. And to stop wasting our life energy and time thinking about those issues, which slow us down and age our bodies. Grudges and regrets are like plaster for the mind. Those thoughts are like viscous vibrations, gluing our mind onto the realm of fear. To escape from this deadly experience, we have to learn to center ourselves from the spirit point, enabling the observation process of the mind, which detaches it gradually from the ego and decreases the prospect of identifying to the issue.

Forgiveness is the process of surrendering to love, to give the mind access to higher constructive thoughts. At this moment, the spirit will take charge of the body and mind by accelerating its healing. You will know when you have totally forgiven, because you will get along with the universal dynamic again, which will attract synchronicities and all sorts of benevolent beings and situations in your life.

Forgiveness is one of the most intense interactions with love. It demands full communication with the soul through your being, as this is a direct contact from the source. It strikes the self and touches the spirit. Nevertheless the soul has to be fully admitted by the spirit, setting aside the ego.

It is an intense spiritual workout, when some emotions are handled by a strong egoistic conviction, unable to move on. This is also creating an organic neurological pathway in the brain, due to its repetitive thinking. The feeling of obsession is pure egotistic intransigence, directing the mind toward unhealthy thinking, and directing the person to be completely led by the emotion of anger.

Grudges and resentments exist only in the ego mind. Forgiveness is a soulful action in order to distract the ego mind from its obsession; while the ego is losing focus, the soul can inject the mind with its loving vibrations, healing the self in this perspective. Once the person is healed, the whole universe rejoices. We are a piece of the universe, and when we understand that we can consciously heal ourselves, we then acknowledge that every time we forgive we are healing a part of the universe too. So we don't have to take things personally, as there is no person as such, but the perspective of one self, expressed as the universe.

CHAPTER 19

———∾◦⟊◦∾———

RELATIONSHIPS
AND THE SELF

*"Greater is He that is in you, than he that is in
the world"*

           - Jesus Christ (Gospel of Thomas)

So, we are made from love and everything
that is part of the universe is the energy of love
materialized or non-materialized.

The mind is the non-materialized part of
consciousness. Consequently, any physical
bodies are the materialized part of the mind in
consciousness.

Consciousness is the communion between the
self and the soul.

The spirit is the emanation of the self, and an extension of it; the self is the body of the soul, and the soul the body of Love. I could go further saying that Love is the "body" of God. It was the Soul's purpose that brought the self to focus. Therefore, your being is one perception of the self: what you call *yourself. The self* is incarnated in the "You" this organic structure, which is by itself an incarnation of the spirit through the mind.

Yourself is what you call your person, from the separation point of view or, if you prefer, from the ego side.

Yes, this organic structure is made of a primary thought, representing a specific perception of the self. It is representing your purpose as a person, as yourself.

And the vehicle that transports "yourself" is what we call our body. Its anatomy and physiology is perfectly organized, as it is directly directed by love energy through the spirit; it has its own mechanism, fitting the purpose in this cosmic dimension. The universe has got many dimensions, and each cosmic body is tailored according to laws and principles of the reality which they have been created in.

Therefore, our anatomy is made for this reality, in this particular universe. The cells of our bodies are wielded by the cosmic rhythm of the universe. They are following its pattern and naturally respond to their functions without troubling the harmony, as they are conscious of the self's purpose. The cells work with the purpose, not for it. They are the purpose in action! They know that, and do what they know best, creating organs, which create a network of different types of functions, all working in synchronicity, for the one purpose serving "yourself".

When you feel good in your body, you actually sense the connection between "yourself" and the organic part of your purpose. Your body is the one from where everything comes through, it is made to take all spiritual experiences into the physical realm. In order for you to feel good in your body, you must first understand this relationship between yourself and your body (the manifested part of the purpose). Nothing could really happen in this reality without this body. Once we have understood that this relationship is the initial relationship for any living beings, we then will start to work harmoniously within this realm.

A positive and loving relationship with ourselves is paramount, prior to any other relationship or action in this world. Without a good relationship between our mind and body, nothing can be achieved with potency. We must cultivate a healthy way of thinking and living, to enhance our inner power in the environment. Our bodies need a constructive and coherent human hood in order to grow healthy and strong.

Many people dismiss this process, as they find it too challenging and disturbing at first. Changing our way of thinking and our neurological pathways is intense and very painful at the beginning, and are even more unlikely to be smooth when our entourage is still living in unconsciousness. Most people give up the idea before even taking any action. They are instead projecting this personal development onto others. We jump from a *"myself- my body relationship"* to a *"yourself- my body relationship"*. When it comes to relationships for instance, sex plays a great part in this projection. Once we have let another body share in our intimacy, we feel suddenly almost obligated to become its shadow. It is true that sexual encounters are very powerful, as they are an exchange of physical energy and mental perceptions - an exchange of love particles.

Sexual intercourse can be highly addictive for the body and the mind, especially if it procures a lot of pleasure. This also creates a neurological pathway in the brain, if the relationship lasts for a while. The fact we want to possess another body, another purpose, causes us to ignore our own spiritual call. Asking someone else to make it happen for us creates more absence between our "self" and our body. It seems that, somehow, we have developed this tendency of swapping our minds into our partner's body, spiritually speaking. Somehow we have come to believe that we must first love someone else before loving ourselves. Eventually, even when we are able to do it, it still feels like an unfulfilled exchange, as it remains lived with conditional love. It does so for as long as our partner can respond with a positive attitude to our emotional requests. But when he or she stops committing to us, this is the end of our "happy" era. We will have to go back to our own mind. All this time spent in someone else's life will have created a void between our purpose and our self, as it has remained unfulfilled during the time of the relationship.

Going back to our self after a rupture, always feels cold and scary at first, and this absence of purpose is interpreted by the ego as loneliness. Also, the ego mind will bombard countless negative thoughts due to its disappointment and insecurities. When this happens, the "Hell Island" isn't far away, showing the tip of its shore on the ocean of the mind. You will find plenty of persons on this island. Actually we can say that the *Hell Island* is our current collective mindset, as this mindset seems to take us away from a peaceful humanity. This vicious spiral can put our purpose on hold for a very long time, if we do not take responsibility for our own part of the self.

So for how long are we going to let our mind down? What would it take for us to become accommodated with the "myself- my body relationship"? When are we finally going to be ready to commit to it before committing to anything or anyone else? I know what you are thinking, that we are all one self, so it shouldn't matter that much if we love someone or something else prior to our personal relationship. Well, yes it does matter, because the self is living through this specific perspective too, and without your presence it cannot bring love to it, therefore one part of the self stays unfulfilled with love. We need to understand that, while we are spending our lives in the perspectives of others, we are spending the same amount of time letting our perspective be filled with void. This void is the lack of our presence in our own lives, in our own self. When someone wants to love you before even loving him or herself it creates a void in the universe, delaying the soul's purpose. You see, this is an eternal dilemma.

The only way to stop this insane loop is to go back to where we come from: ourselves! Once we have established a confident relationship, we can eventually start to spend time in people's realities. This will be effortless and painless, as being in love with ourselves will create a natural positive connection with the environment and other beings, which will take us to be there for them in a very different way. We will love them for who they are and who they are becoming. We will try to encourage each other instead of competing, understanding instead of fighting, appreciating instead of judging, and we will truly love instead of fearing.

Once we make up with ourselves again, we will change the egotistic self into a higher altruistic self. From there will begin the growth of the Being of humanity.

CHAPTER 20

———∿⌇∘⌇ℭ⌇∘⌇ℭ⌇∘⌇∿———

RECONNECTION WITH OUR NATURAL TALENTS

"Our talents are the deepest expression of our Being. It is the rhetoric of life"
- Veronique Bianconi, Body worker,
author and artist (born in 1974)

Becoming a being of humanity is becoming completely who we really are, without the boundaries of the ego mind. We are here with something that we know how to do best. We know it from a very early age, but our societies and our education (parental, institutional) have made us suppress some primary skills. These are gifts, or call them talents, we own from birth. Those talents are a direct heritage from our genetic, but also a spiritual follow up of what we had really enjoyed and mastered on earth, lifetime after lifetime. Unfortunately, this is most of the time ignored by our societies, especially if those skills aren't very conspicuous at first. This is true except for what we call prodigies who show their talents in an obvious way straight from birth.

However, we must know that we are all skilled and talented, but that sometimes more digging work is required before it can become distinct to others and sometimes ourselves. There is time when we feel like doing what we really enjoy and love, but our social system has made us believe that it is not possible to earn a living with our natural birth talents; that only some elites in the field we enjoy can do so. So we are not allowed to practice due to other social commitments and educational purpose imposed upon us, and can only do so for the well-being of our governments. These social commitments started to grow more and more as our civilization strongly focused on earning a living that will provide for the utility bills, the mortgage, the food, clothing, etc…

This system gradually succeeds in suppressing our spiritual connection, letting the ego mind dominate it. We can start to feel a sense of frustration, which can be very subtle, almost imperceptible when very young. Nevertheless this mild frustration will grow with time, especially if we haven't met the social and familial targets dictated in the first place, if we haven't fulfilled the collective agenda. It is then that a real questioning happens within ourselves, making us worry and doubtful about the future.

Many people now are having psychotherapy, physical therapy or simply counseling in many different ways in order to get rid of this doubtful impression inside of us. The stress is now becoming a real social and personal issue, creating mental and physical disorders. That is why in western countries spiritual practices and healthy lifestyles are really taking off. This is because it reconnects us with our greater self, the reality of the heart. It is finally saying in the face of this current paradigm what we all feel or have felt at some point in our lives.

We have triggered this tremendous reality which has strove inside us with a hungry desire for truth. This determination is a statement from the spirit within, a declaration of the inner being. No matter what limited set of beliefs we hold within, the force of love is present and it only depends on one conscious moment, one time to really be in the here and now, enabling our higher self to come forth. Sometimes it takes "extreme" life experiences to take you to the here and now, for example a near death experience, the loss of a loved one, a material loss such as bankruptcy, but also a positive experience, like falling in love, being touched by a beautiful synchronicity, a meaningful situation linking many people together, an interaction with a benevolent or celestial being, the finding of an unknown knowledge, etc... Those are events for the soul, an opportunity to connect with the spirit through the mind and body, it is the fortuity of our inner being.

Chapter 21

—‿◦◦◦◦◦◦‿—

Strategy of the ego

"We must go beyond the constant clamor of ego, beyond the tools of logic and reason, to the still, calm place within us: the realm of the soul"
- Deepak Chopra, Physician, alternative medicine and spiritual author (born in 1947)

Young humans are the future of our society and should be encouraged to become a fruitful being for this humanity. Well, except that our natural connection with our gift, our talent has been mostly ignored or undermined. What we are working with isn't coming from our spirit, but from someone else's ego, which creates a time lapse between yourself and what you are becoming for the sake of this social enterprise, and for the only benefit of the Academy. In this academy, nothing is related to you or your spiritual purpose, but to its collective egotistic mind for its own comfort and control on earth. A great sense of dominance takes place in our everyday life, which even expands in our intimacy and brings up a tenacious feeling of frustration. Deep inside, our spirit is dying to co-create with joy and spontaneity, living out of the love energy to create more connection between beings. We are craving genuine connection between each other and other living organisms.

This frustration is so discernible now, that the healthcare industry is getting overwhelmed with physical and mental illnesses, like a tumor spreading in the body of humanity, trying desperately to avoid the disastrous effects we have created with our small selves. This is now becoming so obvious that we are standing on the edge of the precipice of our time. There are no more places to hide. We are facing each other's frustration almost on a daily basis, affecting our social behaviors and our personal relationships too. The constant exchange of negative information keeps exposing our inadequacy for living in this preposterous matrix. This is not to put down the system, where we are all participating in some extent, but to show that this is not the altruistic way we are currently experiencing, but the collective ego's way and it is reducing what and who we are a little bit more every time. The ego has one obsession: to possess the outer world.

The ego ignores that it is already all of this, and that it is inside the self, or as Jesus would say *"inside the father"*. That is why so many things are controlled by humans, this obsession to make everything man made, instead of letting the earth do its job; we are now growing food in a laboratory, and cloning animal's flesh for the purpose of junk food, all these for business purposes. In these businesses there is no time for natural growth, we must produce something "profitable" to attract people's attention and consequently money. This vacuum of selfishness works for itself at the cost of our health and lives, but also at the cost of other living creatures on earth. The fire alarm has been ringing for a while now, and we cannot ignore it anymore.

Although we see people going down in the streets to protest against those greedy purposes and disclose another way, nevertheless they are still being ignored by the mass population and even treated like criminals by our governments. We see communities of people trying to live out of this corrupted system, whistle-blowers speaking up on different topics, but still we hold on to what we've got, even if what we got isn't the source of our happiness and health. We seem to always find an excuse to close our eyes and play the ostrich game. Yet they are simply pointing out how much we have become conditioned to the human's ego mind, how much personal power and well-being we are sacrificing for governmental recognitions and rewards. Although, we see that all these political enterprises are triggering wars and conflicts, taking away all sorts of freedoms from us and making us witness human, animal and biodiversity massacres, slaughtered by their laws and greed for material values... The suffering we are currently inflicting on ourselves and our environment will soon become uncontrollable, and the spirit is feeling the danger, as it sees this malignant purpose spreading onto other organisms. For example, some research has shown that, due to the high level of toxicity in the environment, some animals have started to develop cancer.

These terrible facts are demonstrating the unconsciousness of some humans who are treating the earth like garbage, using it as a dumping ground for chemical waste. Drastic consequences will arise if we keep resisting our higher purpose, and try to slow down this forthcoming shift. What I mean is that for every action there is a reaction, and the actions we are creating aren't for the benefit of all beings, not even for our own species, therefore the consequences will be related to what we cause.

Unconscious living takes us to irresponsible actions, which takes us to uncaring behaviors, and carelessness is the path to suffering and death.

So let's be aware of the ego's strategy, by taking control of our lives and purpose again, for our own benefit and for all living creatures on Earth.

CHAPTER 22

―――ᴡᴡ◦ᴄ◦ᴇᴇ◦ᴄ◦ᴇ◦ᴏ◦ᴡᴡ―――

DEATH

"The day which we fear as our last is but the birthday of eternity"
- Lucius Annaeus Senaca, Roman
Philosopher and dramatist (4BC-65 AD)

Death in spiritual terms means that the physical body of a being is de-materialized. It remains temporarily unstructured, in the mind field, until a conscious connection is made with love energy again. Obviously in this process, the spirit is supported by other benevolent beings, but mainly it is a perpetuation of our projections within the non-constructed part of the mind. We will go from one lifetime to another, until we fulfilled our part of the purpose that will enable us to love our mind completely. This will bring peace to the being and make it whole with the soul. On some occasions some beings can suspend their incarnations, because they have reached the point of ultimate delusion, meaning that they believe that they have lost their connections with love, by totally identifying to their ego mind. That perception became so strong that it persists beyond the incarnated realm, disabling the spirit and preventing the acknowledgement of any thoughts from love. This spirit lives in the realm of ultimate delusion, the plane of fear. Those entities avoid all constructive or benevolent aspects of themselves or others, as their abilities to appreciate life have turned into a combat against love. This delusional belief can suspend their human's life experience, pausing their incarnations on hold, until loving thoughts touch their minds again.

The influence from fear energy became so strong and real to them, that instead of acknowledging their experiences and retrieving the connection with love, they are instead developing angry and hatred feelings toward it. This makes them drop into darkness a little bit more every time, up to the point that they eventually cut themselves off from the collective aspiration. Certainly this separation is temporary, as we are all part of the self and we are all a piece of the universal purpose, which we are only able to achieve through our own learning pace. Nevertheless this identification to fear lets them be completely manipulated by the ego mind, even at the risk of not reincarnating for a while. Therefore, the only way for those beings to come out from this momentary void would be to feel love energy again. By demonstrating compassion we can inspire them to come forth on the physical plane and carry out the purpose again. Love is always there, but those spirits cannot feel it due to the powerful influence of fear energy upon their minds. Compassion is the only thing that can bring them back to living in an incarnated body.

The love they feel from another being, or from an entire group, is enough for their hearts to "open again" and let the source of life dissolve this energy of fear within them. The more compassion they feel, the more connection they will regain. They must be touched by love gradually, until they succeed to raise their vibrations, and change their minds.

Sometimes some disincarnated beings long to go back to the physical realm, without the love connection. They are still dwelling on the past, as they are living in the ego mind, their small selves having kept alive some desires and greed. Sometimes some memories from previous incarnations are so strong, that they are pushing them to force physical contact at any cost. They go where they know best, and try to take advantage of ignorant or insecure beings by accessing physicality via their minds and, therefore connect to their bodies.

We must understand that by ignoring these high vibrations, which are connections with love and the reality of our higher self, we generate a void. This absence of self-love can become a potential niche for destructive, negative or lonely entities. This process is even more likely to happen with people abusing drugs or alcohol, as these substances affect our physiology and distort our thinking pattern with time. It creates an absence within the being, degrading the vessel and the personal relationship between the spirit and the self, creating the perfect gateway for the dark-minded. Some religions call that possession. But this is a way to also realize that our body is a cosmic vehicle and that, if we don't become a responsible "driver" (the individual part of the spirit), then this body can be taken over by other bodiless entities. There is nothing cruel in this process, as it is also all in the mind.

Once we have realized that we are the being thriving for the purpose to make one with our mind in order to complete the soul, and to see that our physical bodies are an extension of that purpose, then we realize that nothing else is the creator apart from love, and that nothing dies but just transforms. As the French scientist and philosopher Antoine Lavoisier quoted: *"Nothing is lost, everything is transformed"*, therefore if we want to perpetuate greater life experiences, we must acknowledge in our spirit the ultimate connective force in the universe: LOVE.

This connection with love expands consciousness in the mind, generating epiphanies (revelations) in the spirit which leads it to take actions, guided by the being's free will, meaning that this is an active choice of the spirit in this specific perception, a manifestation without the assistance of the divine. This comes from a genuine desire of the spirit to "reconnect" with the source, to love the source. Our spirits yearn to become creative again and to acknowledge any destructive tendencies in order to transcend them. This pure individual action is so important for the universe, as it is pure spiritual emanation unleashing its mighty power into matter.

At that moment we become like gravity for the universe, able to connect matter with love energy in no time. For that to happen, we have to be true to ourselves in order to gain clarity, we have to transcend any illusion in the mind, to let love shines through the spirit and illuminate the world.

Truth is the direct path to love, the one that expresses its deep desire for us to be free from mental constructions and conditioning.

Truth is a direct connection between the metaphysic and physic.

Truth is ultimate clarity

But this process is gradual, as we are under so much conditioning. This is like a mental workout, as the physical body is already directed by love energy at the cellular level.

Reality check:

We can witness our governments having a strong interest in the food industry. This is taken over gradually by the "academy", the agenda is trying to remove the energy of love from our cells, by giving us chemical-based food. By doing so they succeed in suppressing the connection with love energy at the cellular level and in transforming the DNA: **this is very dangerous,** spiritually speaking for the human race, as if they damage our precious bodies, we will spend our time struggling in this karmic realm for a long time, living in separateness all most permanently, and therefore bringing the emotion of loneliness from birth. This would be unbearable and almost impossible for human beings to carry out the purpose, as the conditioning would come from the core. It is already hard now, with a good and healthy body, to reconnect with ourselves. We can feel the benefit of detoxing our bodies or, as religions call it fasting; the necessity to cleanse our physical bodies from all sorts of toxins and parasites. It is the same as if you were in your house and never clean it, after a while it would become unhealthy to live there.

Therefore, it is paramount for all of us to start looking after our own body and its way of alimenting it. Nothing can replace natural fresh food. And if we do not stop this egotist process now, we are setting ourselves up for a living hell: **We have to bring Heaven upon earth and not hell on earth**. We must recognize the signs and act accordingly by becoming conscious thinkers, eaters and drinkers.

Health is not something we can take for granted with age, it is not just a physical process, but it is a coherent communication between body and mind. The mind has to work with the body, not for the body, as the two are the core of this life experience. It is important to make this grammatical difference, which helps to remove the controlling tendency of the ego upon our mind.

There are two ways of living our lives, with dualistic thinking or non-dualistic thinking. Dualistic thinking is the reality of the ego mind within the small self, pertaining to fear vibrations; it is the one that believes in separateness: This creates illusions and boredom.

Non-dualistic thinking is the reality of the alter ego within the higher self, the one that lives in wholeness, pertaining to love vibrations: This reveals truth and purpose.

So death and health are interrelated, on a physical and mental level. It is a state of being within the spirit. An understanding of that the mind and the body are a continuous expression of the spirit within this universe. To look after our physical bodies is to take care of our minds too, and the more awareness we are gaining, the more we are connecting to our spirit, therefore we are bringing forth our inner being on planet Earth, bringing the Being of humanity alive, ready to co-create in the new paradigm.

Chapter 23

---◦~ഊ◦ഏ◐ഏ◦ഊ~◦---

Intuition

"Open to the Heart, value its intuition. Choose to let go of fear, and to open the true and you will awaken to the freedom, clarity and joy of being"

- Mooji, Spiritual teacher, follower
of Papaji, who was a disciple of
Ramana Maharshi (born in 1954)

Being intuitive is simply having a conscious moment, or becoming conscious of that moment. It is being in the moment with maximum awareness. Intuition is the language of the heart. The more conscious we become, the more clarity and presence we gain. As we become conscious of our purpose, we become more intuitive, decreasing rational thinking. This could also develop other brain functions, some parts that have never been used before, as we are limited in the amount of mental activities that we can undertake, when living unconsciously.

The universe is transient and it contracts and expands at times. According to some scientists, the universe is in constant expansion and is accelerating more and more. But the collective mind is also influenced by other universal factors, of which we are unable to be aware simply due to the poor level of consciousness we currently hold.

We must become aware of the different planes we hold in our being. This universe is contained in one perception, or shall we say one specific perception, of the mind, directed by the spirit. Once we acknowledge that we are souls connected by the energy of love, then the natural understanding arises in the mind of that everything is coming from love, and that the universe is by itself the expression of this interaction. Love is the essence of God, and God is the source of life. This awareness will activate intuition in the mind. Bringing a natural connection with the source of life into the constructed world, this can break through the sensation of materiality, interpreted by the ego mind as separation. Intuition is the thinking process of the higher self. It is the grasp of essential thoughts without any fear energy involved. Intuition breaks through the four planes of existence of birth, growth, sickness and death. In other words, intuition is a direct manifestation of the soul plane. It is a direct communication from the spiritual realm to our organisms. Developing our intuition in this world is the act of becoming wired to the spiritual realm.

It is like the Ariadne's string for the being - the Greek mythology of a man, Theseus, who volunteered to go down the Minotaur's labyrinth in order to kill him, and where Ariadne, who was in love with Theseus, gave him a sword and a ball of thread so he could find his way back. Our intuition is there to avoid us getting lost in this very complex structured universe. It is easy to get trapped or lost in those experiences, to forget our purpose when we are involved with the ego mind. Intuition is here to pull us out of this mess and put us back onto the path of our purpose. Intuition is the Ariadne's thread in the labyrinth of our minds.

Chapter 24

—⁓ⲟⲟⲉⲣⲟⲟⲉⲣⲉⲟⲟⲙ—

THE ASCENSION PROCESS

"And Jesus said to them: 'when you pray, say: Father, hallowed be your name. Your Kingdom come'"

- The Bible, Luke 11:2.

Through this ascending process the spirit learns to reconnect with the being, and detaches itself from the ego mind in order to bring forth its alter ego: The higher self. This is in order to transcend from the four planes of existence, and to reconnect the physical body to the spiritual body, through the presence of the higher self.

The small self, our ego, is transforming every time we are gaining consciousness. We are just starting now to be aware of this, as before it was being interpreted as insanity for the person who was ongoing a metaphysical transformation. It is true that this can be very intense for the being to get through it, and it also brings forth a sense of fundamental loneliness at first, triggering a lot of issues onto the surface of the mind, meaning that what was lived on an unconscious level, reveals itself as soon as consciousness arises in the mind to transcend it.

Nevertheless, a period of adjustment is needed for the brain, as it is a real rewiring work for the central nervous system (CNS) and like any healing process, it is painful. Although once triggered, it will get rid of the negative, destructive thinking patterns which are anchored in our bodies and minds. But only faith can enable us to find the strength in maintaining the healing, in order for the being to resist the pain and suffering produced by matter during this spiritual growth. This spiritual experience is the most profound and extraordinary for a being. The ego is so importantly attached to the spirit which will try everything to remain. The illusionary life that the small self has built up around the brain is so present and believed by the body, that it feels almost like death when the ascension process starts to occur.

It is in itself the death of the small self, although what is really happening is the ego transcending into the realm of higher self.

It's like giving birth to a new self, our higher self. But once we manage to get through the organic sensation, we can start to really appreciate and live with the benefits brought up in our lives by this change, and let our actions be directly inspired by our being.

And we start to consciously think from love.

Once the mind has acknowledged that this is a fundamental process, its resistance becomes less, but the pain it generates can put the mind off, at this stage. This ascension can trigger an illness (mental or physical), an accident, a loss (material or emotional), etc... depending on how much resistance we have. It is a real concern for the being and it is understandable, but this is why faith is fundamental. Actually, it is impossible to complete the process of ascension without gaining faith. Faith is there to support the body and mind to ascend with minimal suffering and stress. Faith also brings other ascended beings to our "rescue", they are here to support us, and they can be noticed through synchronized situations or sudden manifestations when needed.

Faith is the primary quality coming from the soul realm right into the mind, to support and assist it with the purpose.

Working with faith is gaining total trust in the universe. This is the knowing that, even if we feel afraid to pursue our calling, something has been triggered inside of us so deeply that it will shape and guide our lives with great deeds. We deeply know what is good to do and what is not, according to our emotional guidance. Intuition works simultaneously with faith: We have faith to become our higher self no matter what is going on in our lives at this present moment. What was happening prior to our epiphany was only linked to the past actions of our small selves, which was limiting us to become the greater version of ourselves.

Anything that is determining us is fear, love brings clarity and expansion.

The ascending period brings a conscious feeling of the source of life within us. It is a real moment of attention by the source, the current dynamic between the universe and the being. The highest intention put into action.

CHAPTER 25

THE GROWTH

"The key to growth is the introduction of higher dimensions of consciousness into our awareness"
- Lao Tzu, Ancient Chinese Philosopher
and poet (604 BC- 531 BC)

Now that we know the different structures of this multi-dimensional being, it is imperative for us to begin the ascension process, as we can see that this will be the next step for all of us, and that we cannot avoid the transcendence into a greater body. This can be observed by the way our societies are currently transforming and communicating. The pace we are reproducing is accelerating, which shows that the body of humanity is quickly growing. We are like the cells of a fetus developing in the womb of mother Earth. This is where the conscious thinking process, the conscious free will come into place. We must not let the fear grasp this body anymore and leave it to create our reality, or we will decline into a very dark, destructive realm, playing a negative role for the universe, an entity that always runs away from the best things in life, befriending with toxic organisms until its total destruction.

That is why compassion is present in order for us to retrieve this connection, to be inspired by other loving spirits who can make us feel loved again, so we can link our individual perspective to the whole. It is necessary to bond between us in order to collectively channel love energy. This bond is like the connective tissue of humanity, linking every body and mind.

Our physical body is our house, our home, hosting our being, it is the vehicle through which the universe communicates and transmits life, in order for the soul to work through the mind.

We must love our mind!

Without a loved mind we cannot carry noble ideas, constructive thoughts or insightful knowledge, and neither can we maintain a healthy and fit body. If the mind is not working with the body for a great achievement which can provide elevation and coherent thinking, then it will bring suffering and chaos to this world. We must also begin to acknowledge that we are not only liable to ourselves but to other creatures too, as we shouldn't forget that we are actually all one self, expressing itself through different perspectives.

The higher self is there to connect us to the non-dual part of the self, for the purpose of co-creation and ascension. With the awareness of wholeness, we are able to carry out this greater life experience from living to being.

CHAPTER 26

———ᘑᘉᘈᗑᗒᘈᘉᘑ———

PERCEPTION

"Most of our troubles are due to our passionate desire for and attachment to things that we misapprehend as enduring entities"
- Dalai Lama, Current Dalai Lama,
head monks of the Tibetan Buddhist Gelug
school and Nobel prize (born in 1935)

As quantum physics has explained it, the microcosm and the macrocosm is a reflection of the whole, it is all about perspectives. For example, if you have lived all your life in the same town, and never been on a plane, you may never feel or see the bigger scale of your birth place. You live and think with a tiny perspective of your town, making you believe that everything is far from each other, and which could limit your faculty to co-create, as you have never experienced its bigger scale. But, as soon as you start traveling, you will see that this is not the case. You will see that everything is interconnected, that your community is not so inaccessible and that it could just be a matter of determination more than a geographical problem.

The scale where we stand is what can be brought into a higher perspective. When we are getting emotionally or physically involved in something or with someone, it narrows our scales, our views, and obstructs the rest of the universe during the time of identification. This brings a sense of disconnection, which can develop into feelings of insecurity, and therefore keep us stuck where or with who we are, this is called attachment. Attachment is the by-product of insecurity. The fear of the unknown makes us forget that there are no unknowns, but only parts of us not yet experienced. "Knowing thyself" is the most precious gift we have yet to offer to our being. This knowing removes those insecurities within us, and unblocks the mind, letting the source of life flow freely inside us.

We have to practice the art of detachment without losing the connection with love. We have to become more conscious without the thinking process limiting the performance. It is part of this life experience to get involved, to dive temporarily into the depth of our lifetime reality. But we must be equipped with high flexible feelings, like thick elastic strings attached to a puppet, enabling us to elevate ourselves when the experience implies deep, strong emotions.

To have a clear insight of our possible attachments prior to the involvement is paramount for the being, if we want to thrive in the reality of the higher self. This can sound scary for the ego mind and can feel like an impossible work to do on a constant basis. It is true that it is hard work at first, but if we want to evolve we have to break through this conditioning maintained by the ego on a personal and collective level.

To break through this unconscious free will and enter the realm of conscious free will, we must start to connect with each other and share our life experiences for the purpose of co-creation and not co-dependency, so we can create a social bond, strengthening it with encouragement, praise and honesty. This bond can be developed and strengthened by using our greater gifts and skills for the sake of our social and personal development. When we do something we love, something we are gifted to do, it doesn't feel like an effort for the mind and body, instead it feels like a satisfaction, and this feeling brings peace to the mind and well-being to the body. This coevality is the fundamental basis for a balanced being and a harmonious society.

In doing what we enjoy and know best, without a constant intellectual effort from the brain, we must listen to our heart's desires and put our talents into practice every day. We must also be able to observe our minds. By observing, we see the energy of love removing linear time from the mind whilst, in contrast, fear reinforces it. Like Albert Einstein demonstrated to us, time is relative to our mind state and physical experience, when our being is involved in something it enjoys, linear time decreases, leaving the sensation of a flowing moment. This gives pleasure to the body and peace to the mind. The same applies when we get involved with something unpleasant linear time increases, and the experience brings pain to the body and suffering to the mind. It traps the spirit into matter.

To be aware of this principle is gaining insight on the power of love. It is realizing that, without love, we wouldn't be able to survive long, as the whole physical experience would become unbearable, unlivable and therefore non-existent. It is also to say that, without love, physicality wouldn't exist, as everything is made of energy.

Energy is the potent manifestation of what we call LOVE.

Our true self is our inner being, and is directly coming from the soul, created by love. To become the being of humanity is to become a caring proactive and conscious spirit, dedicated to the well-being of all and to the expansion of love in this universe. So let's start to be ourselves, let's start to be in love...

"If we have no peace, it is because we have forgotten that we belong to each other"
- Mother Teresa, Roman Catholic religious
sister and missionary (1910-1997).